ART FOR THE PEOPLE

Art for the People

Culture in the Slums of Late Victorian Britain

Edited by Giles Waterfield

DULWICH PICTURE GALLERY

Contents

Foreword

Over a hundred years ago the South London Gallery was built to house a collection of paintings by eminent artists of the day. The paintings were largely donated to the collection by the artists themselves or by wealthy benefactors and it was formed with the intention of providing working people with the opportunity to see the best art being produced at that time. From 1891 until the outbreak of the Second World War in 1939 the collection was permanently on show to the public. During the war the Gallery was closed and one of its two main galleries was destroyed in the Blitz. When the South London Gallery reopened in 1949, with its exhibiting space cut in half, it did so with a new policy, to mount changing temporary exhibitions from outside the collection. From then on works from the collection have been seen only occasionally even though, ironically, it was added to most during the 1950s and 1960s. The Libraries Committee of the then Borough of Camberwell, prompted by the accession of Queen Elizabeth II, authorised the purchase of new additions to the collection. The modern print collection was begun in 1960 and although by the end of the decade the buying of prints had virtually stopped, the print collection now contains some seven hundred works.

Over the years the collection has suffered from neglect, although there are still plenty of local people who remember seeing it in its heyday. It is therefore of real importance that the most signifi-cant works from the collection are on exhibition, newly restored, at Dulwich Picture Gallery, a gallery in which these paintings can be seen to their best advantage in a setting similar to that for which they were originally intended. This collaboration between the South London Gallery and Dulwich Picture Gallery provides the best of both worlds, an opportunity to see some fine paintings in a perfect setting in Southwark, where they were originally intended to be seen.

Now, as the economic climate changes, the London Borough of Southwark is going to add to its collection once more and will begin soon to purchase paintings and prints for the enjoyment of local people. These works will be shown throughout the Borough in schools, hospitals, leisure centres and so on and will provide Southwark with a rich, up-to-date source of visual art. I hope that this collaboration between Dulwich Picture Gallery and the South London Gallery is the beginning of a lasting and fruitful relationship in which the people of Southwark will have access to the best art of the past complemented by the best art of today. We are grateful to Dulwich Picture Gallery for the inspiration for this exhibition and for the opportunity to display these paintings which are part of Southwark's heritage.

Jeremy Fraser
Leader of the Council, London Borough of Southwark

Introduction

This exhibition gives the public the opportunity to view an interesting but little-known collection, and to consider its remarkable history. In its earliest days, the South London Art Gallery (now known as the South London Gallery) was intended to provide opportunities for the enjoyment of the arts for a deprived urban public which otherwise enjoyed few such opportunities. Whatever our modern view may be of the methods used to achieve this aim, such rare enterprises as the South London Art Gallery pioneered the development of museum and gallery education of a new sort: not just for artists or for the cultivated, but for the whole population.

Dulwich Picture Gallery has a long tradition of collaboration with the London Borough of Southwark, which has supported our education programme here since 1989, a programme which, we believe, maintains the best traditions of the old South London Art Gallery. I am delighted that for the first time we have been able to collaborate in the organisation of an exhibition assisted by the help of the London Borough of Southwark and especially of Jeremy Fraser, Leader of the Council, and Stephen Wray, Director of Leisure. It has been a pleasure to work with the staff of the South London Gallery, notably David Thorp and Julian Wakeling.

We have received most welcome help from a number of sources in the funding of the exhibition, especially the Friends of Dulwich Picture Gallery, the Paul Mellon Foundation and the Royal Historical Society acting as Trustees of the Robinson Bequest.

Lenders to the exhibition have been extremely helpful and illuminating. I wish particularly to acknowledge the contribution made by David Allen, Janet Barnes, James Brock, Tom Clarkson, Melva Croal, Emma Davidson, Caroline Ellis, Nicholas Malton, Sandra Martin and Tom Maxwell. In addition, all the authors have made a most valuable contribution to the catalogue and I would like to thank Caroline Arscott, Leonee Ormond and Nicola Smith for their interest in this project. On behalf of the Southwark Local Studies Library, Stephen Humphrey has contributed valuable support, as have his colleagues.

David Collins of the Paper Conservation Department at Camberwell School of Art has provided invaluable assistance. As we have come to expect, Barry Viney has been able, within severe time limits, to design an elegant and appropriate catalogue. The members of Dulwich Decorative and Fine Art Society and North Kent Decorative and Fine Art Society give vital voluntary support in manning the exhibition.

As always I am greatly indebted to the dynamic and imaginative energy of those at Dulwich Picture Gallery, especially Victoria Bethell, Kate Bignold, Sheila Gair, Alan Kaill, Kate Knowles, Charles Leggatt, Sophie Plender, Nicole Ryder, Julian Spicer and Peter Theobald. A number of student volunteers have carried out valuable research and administrative work and I would like to thank Joanne Carpenter, Brett Dolman, Caroline Eason, Kate Goodwin, Emma Hardy, Catherine Houghton, Ben Tufnell and Emma Wigmore. I am particularly grateful for the help I have received from Robert Maniura, Temporary Assistant Curator, without whom the exhibition could not have happened.

Giles Waterfield
Director, Dulwich Picture Gallery

View of South London Art Gallery, c.1900.

Nicola Smith

A Brief Account of the Origins of the South London Art Gallery

The title of the South London Art Gallery is striking. It lays claim not only to Camberwell or Peckham, its immediate environs in the South East, but to the whole of London south of the Thames. This geographical scope is by no means arbitrary; it reveals the insight and vision of the Gallery's founder, William Rossiter. Writing on the occasion of the Gallery's twenty-fifth anniversary in 1893, Rossiter told of his enthusiasm for the work of the first Working Men's College, founded in 1854, and his realisation that many of the students lived in South London 'which is, as I then perceived for the first time, the vast dormitory of the great majority of the men who work in central London . . . From this came the idea of a college in South London, in the midst of the workers'.[1] It was from this College that the Gallery developed and Rossiter's dream was to see it grow into nothing less than 'the National Gallery of South London . . . placed where it is most wanted, where the daily lives of the people most need such refreshment, and where the great artisan class, whose work beautifies the wealthier part of the metropolis, live with so little beauty either natural or derived from art'.[2]

William Rossiter remains a mysterious figure. Born in the parish of St Andrew, Holborn in 1831, the son of a portmanteau maker,[3] by 1851 he was established as a trunk maker at 15 Greville Street in the same parish, apparently working for his father.[4] He married Elizabeth, an orphan living with relatives in London, in 1857.[5] By the late 1860s Rossiter had clearly advanced his education considerably, probably at the Working Men's College in Great Ormond Street nearby, and he emerges as a teacher and author of text books.[6] Works on mathematics and botany and a dictionary of scientific terms are among his surviving

works, published between 1865 and 1873. At this period Rossiter joined a number of learned societies, perhaps to enhance his new academic status. He joined the Royal Geographical Society in March 1867, the Astronomical Society in 1868 and the Chemical Society in 1869.

Rossiter became a teacher at the Working Men's College[7] and it was here that his ideas for a similar institution in South London took shape. The South London Working Men's College opened in 1868 at 91 Blackfriars Road with Rossiter as the manager. In 1878 the College moved to 143 Kennington Lane, which provided larger premises. The College was extended to include a free library, the first in South London. The Library opened in October 1878, and a few months later Rossiter added to it 'by borrowing pictures to cover the walls during the summer months'.[8] The Gallery was born. As time passed the focus of the institution shifted firmly in the direction of the visual arts and this change was explicitly recognised. As Rossiter explained 'so many friends lent pictures, and so many were allowed to remain, that the exhibition intended for a few weeks has now been in existence for about fourteen years, and has become so important that the name of Free Library has been replaced by that of South London Fine Art Gallery'.[9] The original educational role was never forgotten, however, and in 1882 a series of Sunday lectures was inaugurated which remained an important feature of the Gallery's work.[10]

Mention should be made of Elizabeth Rossiter's activity. From 1866 onwards she began taking groups of poor children on trips into the country and in 1877 launched her project of offering free holidays of a fortnight to deserving cases by advertising in the press. The invitation seemed so

MR. ROSSITER.

MRS. ROSSITER.

improbable that Punch reprinted the letter as if it were a joke.[11] The project prospered, however, and constituted an essential complement to her husband's efforts. No more than the Barnetts in Whitechapel did the Rossiters 'expect to regenerate the world by their picture shows'.[12] The Gallery was but a part of a larger endeavour. As a contemporary newspaper report commented: 'Thus, with the other efforts made by Mr. Rossiter, the desires of our humbler brethren – men, women, and children – for a larger, wider, and better life are endeavoured to be met.'[13]

It was Rossiter's policy not to stay in an area once the Free Library Act had been adopted. When Lambeth adopted the Act in 1884 the Gallery moved to Battersea and in 1887 they moved again, this time to Camberwell, 'a thoroughly artisan and neglected neighbourhood, remarkable for the number of its public houses and the vigour of its language; for the long hours of labour and the utter absence of any means of education beyond the day schools; for the enormous number of its children, and for their uncivilized behaviour'.[14] The parish of Camberwell at this date was a place of great contrasts. Dulwich was, as it still is, a wealthy neighbourhood, but around the Surrey Canal, in what is now Burgess Park, was an area of great poverty. The streets around Sultan Street, off Camberwell New Road, were described by Charles Booth as 'in some ways without counterpart in London. There are places more squalid, and there may be people more debased, but there are none whereon the word "outcast" is so deeply branded'.[15] The Gallery had moved to the very heart of the 'great intellectual desert'[16] of South London.

In these early years the Gallery could boast significant success, achieved largely through the determination and tenacity of the individuals involved. The challenges and rewards were described in a speech given by Rossiter at a fundraising function in 1890:

'When we opened new exhibitions in Kennington Lane, at Battersea, at Camberwell, for the first six months our lives were filled with terrors. There was a general supposition amongst the people that everybody who came into the neighbourhood wanted to get something out of it, and – well we did get something. We got cabbage stumps shied at our heads; the children . . . came and swore at us, and little boys of three or four years would want us to fight. I have been invited by a gentleman of four to go out and have my head punched . . . Whenever we opened a new gallery we had twelve months' suffering; three months' dread of what would be done to us; six months suffering of what was done; and three months of gradual recovery. But the benefit of a permanent institution such as ours, going on year after year, is made apparent. We have been able to help those very swearing young monkeys who came to us, we have been able to watch them year after year, because they came day by day – we have been able to watch them growing up into youths, and after 20 years' working I can trace at least 100 people who have passed through the gradations of beginning by swearing at us and throwing cabbage stumps at our heads, then becoming interested, regular attendants at our lectures, and growing and developing into really thoughtful people.'[17]

The efforts made on an individual basis are typified by the new secretary Mary Olver, appointed in 1884, who engaged in direct methods of encouraging visitors:

'If a poor little ragged monkey, seven or eight years of age, dressed in a pair of tattered trousers, part of a shirt and one brace, looks in at the door, he is asked to come in; he looks curiously and is again invited, and then Miss Olver goes and pulls him in. Really, Miss Olver does go out into the highways and compel the people to come in a way that perhaps is not done anywhere else in the kingdom.'[18]

The reward for this tenacity was a spectacular rise in attendance figures. The annual reports show the number of visitors increasing from 27,000 in 1881 to 58,000 in 1886 and 86,500 in 1887.[19]

The Gallery's first location in Camberwell was 207 Camberwell Road, an old glass warehouse. Rossiter was dissatisfied with the accommodation and concerned by the risk of fire. He felt, with some justification, that the Gallery 'small and poor as it was . . . had in it the germ of a great work, a work altogether beyond the small means and poor accommodation which then cramped it. That this germ might not be stifled . . . I appealed to Sir F. Leighton, Mr. Watts, and Mr. Burne-Jones'.[20] This decision in 1887 marked a turning point in the Gallery's history and, as Rossiter was soon to find, brought a fundamental, though perhaps unanticipated, change in his own relationship with the Gallery.

Even with the support of the famous names that now graced the Council of the Gallery, fund-raising was a slow and difficult process. In 1889 Rossiter bought the freehold of Portland House, an imposing building on Peckham Road, for £2,400. He moved into the house and the construction of the new Gallery was begun in the grounds.

Progress on the building works was interrupted by lack of funds. Most seriously an anonymous donor, who had offered to finance the cost of the new building and to provide an endowment of £6,000, pulled out giving only £500. Lady Burne-Jones, another Council member, could only express frustration: 'I went there today myself, and found a rather impressive looking place carried as far as the roof should have been put on and there stopped as if by a spell. It is enough to make anyone who lives there gnash his teeth to think of this beautiful weather all gone to waste and now fog and rain to delay everything.'[21]

The new Gallery in Peckham Road was finally opened to the public in May 1891, the Council having stepped in to meet some of the shortfall, but the Gallery remained, on completion, 'in part the involuntary gift of the builders.'[22] It then closed for two months because of problems with the floor, but reopened in early September. A formal opening ceremony in the presence of the Duke and Duchess of Fife was held in November.

Fund-raising continued. At the Annual General Meeting in 1892 Passmore Edwards, the well-

13

The Ruskin Gallery, c.1900.

Below: The Engraving Gallery, c.1900.

14

known philanthropist and patron of public libraries, offered £3,000 for a new lecture room and library, and G. F. Watts agreed to lay the new foundation stone of the new buildings. The opening ceremony took place on 21 March 1893. According to the *South London Press*'s report, Passmore Edwards 'said that if it were not that the gallery was open on Sundays he should not have made his offer. They must liberalise and emancipate their Sundays . . . At the meeting to which the chairman referred, what particularly struck him was, first that the gallery was free; secondly that it was open on Sundays (and if it were not he should not have helped it); and thirdly, that little children brought in from the streets received there not only instruction but recreation'. Watts in his reply, 'express[ed] a hope that the very youngest children would be admitted to the gallery . . . The taste for art could not be developed too early in a nation like ours . . . Art was not everything but it had a great deal to do; he thought it much to be regretted that our people wanted a taste for art'.[23]

An important source of regular funding was the City Parochial Trustees, a body which distributed money from charities in the City of London to educational causes. From 1891 the Gallery received an annual grant of £300. Their support, however, was conditional and they were not happy with the organisation of the Gallery. Their problem seems to have been Rossiter, who, for all his missionary zeal, was no diplomat and had only a rudimentary grasp of matters of law. They were particularly concerned by remarks that he made in the press 'to the effect that this gallery was not a public institution'.[24] Rossiter also consistently refused to acknowledge the need to revise the Gallery's trust deed to permit the inclusion of two representatives of the City Parochial Trustees on the Council; this was one of the conditions of their continued financial support.

As Leonee Ormond describes, it fell to Lord Leighton to negotiate with the recalcitrant Rossiter. Despite these difficulties, in October 1893 the new part of the Gallery, designed by Sir Ernest George of the well-known firm George and Peto, was officially opened by the Prince of Wales and the Duke and Duchess of York. The Central Library opposite was opened on the same day.

Negotiations continued with the City Parochial Trustees throughout 1894. The City Parochial Trustees were concerned about two points. The first was the ownership of the property and Mr Rossiter's claims upon it. The Gallery belonged to the Trustees but the adjoining Portland House belonged to Rossiter and was rented to the Gallery. If the Gallery were to make applications for public funds all property should belong absolutely to it, with no private claims. The City Parochial Trustees were willing to provide the money for the Trustees to buy out Rossiter's interest, and until this was done the Gallery could not be considered a public institution.

The second problem was Rossiter's position. He was the chief salaried officer, one of only three Trustees and Treasurer. The trust deed made him practically irremovable as Treasurer and Director for life. The City Parochial Trustees wanted a third trustee to be nominated to replace Rossiter, and an independent Treasurer. By the end of 1894 Leighton's patience had run out, and he was considering ways of getting rid of Rossiter.

Leighton seems to have taken his problems next to the Charity Commission, and came up with an agreement between the Council of the Gallery and Rossiter whereby the Gallery would buy Rossiter out. Leighton approached the City Parochial Trustees to provide the money for the buyout.

The matter of the Gallery was first presented to the Vestry of Camberwell in August 1895, when it reported that the Council had approached the Vestry to nominate new members. Clearly the Council members had decided to ask the Vestry for help with their problems, because the next report of the Libraries Committee included a report of a Committee appointed to consider a proposal to transfer the management of the South London Fine Art Gallery to the Local Authorities. The report concluded that the Gallery had outgrown the dimensions originally envisaged and that there was a danger that the resources represented by its buildings might be wasted. Referring to the provisions of the trust deed whereby the

15

The Passmore Edwards Gallery, c.1900.

Gallery might be used as a Reading Room, Lecture Hall 'and generally to promote acquaintance with art, science, and literature among the inhabitants of South London' it recommended that the ownership of the Gallery be transferred to the Commissioners of Public Libraries and Museums of Camberwell to be maintained 'subject to the purpose for which it was founded, viz. to be a Picture Gallery for the people of south London, open to the public free, and on Sundays'. The life tenures of Rossiter and Miss Olver were acknowledged but provisions were proposed for their retirement including the circumstance in which 'the development of the Institution under the new management will require from the Director and Secretary more onerous duties than Mr Rossiter and Miss Olver could reasonably be expected to perform'.

The negotiations were long and complicated and it seems that Rossiter resisted for as long as possible. In December 1895 the Finance and General Purposes Committee of the City Parochial Trustees reported that the Commissioners of Public Libraries and Museums for the parish of Camberwell were prepared to take over the running of the Gallery from the Council for the Gallery and fund it from the library rate provided that it came to them unencumbered by debt, or presumably by Rossiter and Miss Olver. The Library Commissioners wanted over £4,000 to free the Gallery from encumbrances and to purchase the freehold of Gallery and Library and Portland House. Compensation and a retiring allowance for Rossiter, and an annuity for Miss Olver, were also sought. If they received these contributions the Commissioners undertook not to ask for an annual grant. These terms were eventually agreed and the Vestry of St Giles, later the Metropolitan Borough of Camberwell and now the London Borough of Southwark, took over the running of the Gallery.

The purchase of Portland House cleared the way for the final addition to the fabric of the Gallery when, aided again by Passmore Edwards, a new entrance from the street was built to the designs of Maurice Adams. This scheme provided office space for the Gallery and linked it to the newly-founded Camberwell School of Art. The new buildings were opened in January 1898 by Sir Edward Poynter.

The somewhat acrimonious end to William Rossiter's involvement in the South London Art Gallery should not be allowed to diminish his achievement. Moved by a 'great idea . . . the total abolition of poverty both of mind and body, and that not from without but by developing strength from within',[25] he struggled to establish the Gallery in the face of considerable difficulties. Although he seemed to lose touch with the administrative realities of the growing Gallery, to the exasperation of the Council, he can be credited with having acknowledged that the realisation of his vision required more resources than he could muster alone. Yet the loss of personal control came as a harsh blow. Rossiter once remarked of the origin of the Free Library: 'Why, I just threw open the doors of my house and said in effect, "There are my books"'. Until 1887 the Gallery retained this makeshift, almost spontaneous character, 'housed in an ordinary house and shop',[26] but once the powerful characters of the Council stepped in this was bound to change. It is difficult not to read in Rossiter's remarks at the Gallery's twenty-fifth anniversary a regret beyond his overt concern: 'Had I known how readily this help would be given; how much time, and thought, and help in every way, these men would give; how great a tax upon their time and powers they would readily, cheerfully pay, I should have hesitated before asking them.'[27]

FOOTNOTES

1. William Rossiter, *A Summary of the History of the South London Art Gallery, Library and Lecture Hall, from its Foundation in 1868, a Quarter of a Century Ago*, 1893, p.2.
2. Rossiter, 1893, p.5.
3. International Genealogical Index.
4. Census for 1851, Public Record Office.
5. Catalogue of the Works of Art in the Gallery, South London Art Gallery and Lecture Hall, 1895, p.22.
6. Rossiter is listed as a teacher of mathematics and languages in the *London Directory* of 1868, where his address is given as 11 Greville Street. A Henry Rossiter, portmanteau maker, is listed at the same address. Rossiter gives his occupation as teacher in his return for the 1871 census (Public Record Office RG10 592 21 1a 1 f27, p.27). The age given by Rossiter in 1871 is consistent with a birth date in 1831. The correspondence of age, residence and the continuity of the family trade seem to confirm the identity of the individual mentioned in the earlier references with the South London Art Gallery Rossiter.
7. Rossiter described himself as a 'member' of the college from the time of the inaugural lecture onwards. Presumably some of this time was as a student. Rossiter, 1893, p.2.
8. ibid, p.3.
9. ibid.
10. ibid, p.4.
11. S. L. A. G., 1895, p.22.
12. 'At the East-End "Academy". A "Private View" at St. Jude's Schools, Whitechapel.', *Pall Mall Gazette*, 28 April 1886.
13. 'Art and Literature for the People. An Interview with Mr. Wm. Rossiter'.
14. South London Fine Art Gallery and Free Library, Report for 1887, p.4.
15. Charles Booth, *Life and Labour of the People in London. 3rd Series: Religious Influences. Outer South London*, 1902.
16. Rossiter, 1893, p.6.
17. South London Fine Art Gallery, Report of a Public Meeting held on 18 July 1890, p.5.
18. ibid, p.6.
19. S. L. A. G., Report for 1886, p.2, and Report for 1887, p.2.
20. Rossiter, 1893, p.5.
21. Lady Georgina Burne-Jones, letters to J. W. Cross, September to October 1890, Southwark Local Studies Library ms.
22. S. L. A. G., Report for 1891, p.2.
23. *South London Press*, 25 March 1893.
24. City of London Parochial Trustees, Central Governing Body Minutes, 15 May 1893, Guildhall Library ms 8966/1.
25. S. L. A. G., 1890, p.6.
26. Rossiter, 1893, p.5.
27. ibid.

Lord Leighton (photo by R. W. Robinson).

Leonee Ormond

A Leighton Memorial:
Frederic Leighton and the South London Art Gallery

From the beginning, the South London Art Gallery had powerful backers and patrons, recruited by Rossiter. The first Principal of his South London College was Professor Thomas Henry Huxley, and the first President of the Council of the College and Art Gallery was William Ewart Gladstone. In 1887, Gladstone handed over his role to Sir Frederic Leighton, since 1878 President of the Royal Academy. The purpose of this paper is to examine the role played by Leighton and his circle of artist friends in the creation of the South London Art Gallery.

Leighton was no mere figurehead. Trained at the Städel Institute in Frankfurt, he had imbibed there a strong belief in the duty of artists to the community as a whole. Germany represented a leading force in the nineteenth-century drive to build new museums and art galleries for the enlightenment of the general public, an ideal to which Leighton was deeply committed. He was a trustee of the new National Portrait Gallery, was involved in the early plans for the Tate Gallery, and through his friend, Lord Carlisle, influenced the purchasing policy of the National Gallery.

In 1870 Leighton was the main inaugurator of the Winter Exhibitions of the Royal Academy, where Old Masters (often from country houses and other private collections) were shown. Before this Londoners wishing to see great paintings had been restricted to the National Gallery (by no means on the same scale as today), the Dulwich College Picture Gallery (as it then was), a part of the Royal Collection at Hampton Court and, for the middle classes, the picture galleries of a few aristocratic town houses. In order to guarantee the high quality of the Academy's Winter Exhibitions, Leighton twisted the arms of his friends in per-suading them to lend. Few could resist him.

Once elected President of the Royal Academy, Leighton found even greater opportunities to put his beliefs into practice. The minutes of the Academy Council show his close concern with all details of public access, from the formation of a response to the coming of the underground rail-way, to the provision of a ladies' cloakroom. Like everyone else closely involved in bringing the South London scheme into being, Leighton was convinced of the importance of opening the Gallery on Sundays, the only day when most working people would be able to go there.

The South London Art Gallery appointment was a new challenge for Leighton. The Council as a whole was proud of the Gallery's position as the only place (Dulwich excepted) where works of art were on display south of the Thames. Even when the task was particularly arduous, Leighton described the Gallery to a friend as 'a struggling but I am happy to say growing Institution to which I am much devoted in Camberwell'.[1]

Leighton was an excellent holder of the chair at any meeting, manipulative, but with a firm grasp of the issues, and a graceful manner which partially concealed the exercise of power. When he took over the Presidency of the Gallery Council, Leighton seems to have appointed a number of fellow artists to the board. His deputy was Sir James Drumgole Linton, a watercolourist and historical painter, who had been knighted in 1885. Leighton had worsted no less an opponent than Queen Victoria in 1882, when he insisted that Linton be properly paid for his *Wedding of Prince Leopold*. At the same time, he had smoothly intimated to the artist that he should not demand *twice* the sum suggested by the Queen. Leighton's

E. Burne-Jones (oil by P. Burne-Jones, N.P.G., London).

letters to Linton survive, and reveal the President's increasing dependence upon him for support in the affairs of the Gallery.

Other artists appointed to the board were Ernest Crofts, well-known for his battle pieces and an Associate of the Royal Academy, and the Honourable John Collier, then in his late thirties and establishing a reputation for portraits, history paintings and subject pictures of modern life. Walter Crane was an illustrator and painter of mythological subjects, but his interest in the South London Art Gallery had more to do with his social-ist impulses, fostered under the influence of William Morris. Also associated with Morris, but apolitical, was Edward Burne-Jones. An active Council member was Wyke Bayliss, recently elected President of the Royal Society of British Artists, and a writer with a strong interest in archi-tecture. Bayliss, knighted in 1897, was one of the Gallery's most active supporters.

By 1890, Leighton had brought three new members onto the Council: his friend and neigh-bour, George Frederic Watts, Watts' wife, Mary, and Burne-Jones's wife, Georgiana. This move played a large part not only in the survival of the Gallery, but, for the time being at least, in the survival of its President. Much of the practical work of fund-raising and administration was done by Georgie Burne-Jones. Leighton, unmarried and apparently without any powerful sexual orien-tation, was well aware of the potential abilities of women, even though, under the influence of his sister, Alexandra Sutherland Orr, he had once tried (unsuccessfully) to recruit Mary Watts for the anti-suffrage campaign.

Watts and his wife had both been involved with philanthropic work in Whitechapel before their marriage, Watts helping a Whitechapel clergy-man, Canon Barnett, to encourage a love of art among his parishioners, and Mary Fraser Tytler teaching modelling to Whitechapel people. Watts never forgot his own impoverished boyhood and was committed to assisting others, particularly those with artistic impulses. Both Watts and Leighton were neighbours of the redoubtable Emilie Russell Barrington, also deeply involved in the Whitechapel scheme. It was probably through Mrs Barrington that Leighton was drawn into the John Kyrle Society, named in tribute to the 'Man of Ross', and dedicated to opening up 'beautiful places' to the poor.

In pursuit of this ideal, those whom Leighton referred to as the Whitechapellians visited his house with its remarkable Arab Hall at least once a year, usually when Leighton himself was either abroad or away from home: 'they may see every-thing except the studio', he told Emilie Barring-ton in 1885.[2] Watts' house was also opened to them, and Leighton told Mary Watts:

'I am sincerely glad that our friends from the East received pleasure from their visit to Kens-ington. I think it is not without its uses that they should see, also, things which are delight-ful in the way of decorated architecture, because if they like them, it can only be on

G. F. Watts (photo by J. P. Mayall).

<u>artistic</u> grounds or something akin to them; in our <u>pictures</u>, if they like them, it is, be assured, never <u>the art</u> which touches them.'[3]

Appropriately, a group of Leighton's Kyrle Society letters was published in 1903 and sold in support of the Leighton House maintenance fund.

A common philanthropic impulse was only one point of connection between the artists on the South London Art Gallery Council. Crane's mosaics were an important feature in Leighton's Arab Hall, while Watts painted portraits of Leighton, Crane and Burne-Jones. Crane advised Mary Watts on her 'gesso' ceiling for Watts' new house in Surrey, Limnerslease.

However idealistic this group may have been, their work at the South London Art Gallery forced them to take practical measures, and to recognise the overwhelming importance of raising money, without which the scheme would undoubtedly fail.

The major problem to which the Council had to address itself was how to fund a new building. In 1889, when the Gallery moved to its present site, the first intention was to make one room fire-proof, so that the pictures could be shown, and then to build an exhibition area beside the house. For the current exhibition, Leighton stated that he would be lending some of his own works for the show from August until October. He appealed for further loans.

By October an average of 4,000 had visited the Gallery on weekdays with 2,000 on Sundays. As onlookers reported, these were genuine working people. Among those who had lent works were members of the Council and other artist friends of Leighton including Philip Hermogenes Calderon and Marcus Stone. Among the private owners who responded to the President's call was the Baroness Burdett Coutts, so well known for her philanthropy that the gesture caught the attention of the

Angela Burdett-Coutts (watercolour by W. C. Ross, N.P.G., London).

press. The loans from her collection, presumably those works still in the Gallery in 1895, were a mixed group, with a copy of a Murillo, a Lawrence portrait, two seascapes, twenty drawings of South Wales, and a number of views of two of the Baroness's major charitable schemes, Columbia Square and Columbia Market, Bethnal Green. These last were apparently the work of the Baroness's architect, H. A. Darbishire.[4]

By this time, Leighton's burden was not so much financial as personal. Controlled and courteous at all times, he regularly came near to bursting point when dealing with Rossiter. According to Mary Watts: 'Sir Frederic told me that the work connected with the Gallery had cost more time and labour than the affairs of the Academy had ever entailed.'[5] Leighton was, above all else, per-

sistent, and, during the eight or so years of acquaintance, he persisted in trying to make Rossiter understand what was meant, and what, in Leighton's view, was best for the Gallery. Mary Watts saw 'a large-sized portmanteau absolutely filled by letters' from Leighton in Rossiter's office.[6] Walter Crane remembered how Leighton 'helped to pilot the institution from the somewhat exacting proprietorship of its founder towards its ultimate position as a public institution'.[7]

One source of friction between Rossiter and Leighton lay in a simple personality clash. The elegant Leighton and the battling Rossiter were unlikely to see eye to eye on methods of raising money or of organisation. Rossiter was direct in manner, used to pursuing his own way, a true reformer and pioneer. Leighton was an odd mixture of idealism and pragmatism. He held powerful beliefs, but, at the same time, worked with practical intelligence to put them into effect. This split in attitudes was clearly expressed (if in Leighton's absence) at a public meeting in July 1890. Henry Irving, giving an address on behalf of the Gallery, referred to Watts, Burne-Jones and Leighton as those 'whose pictures have carried visions of ideal form and colour into many a soul which never before had any perception of the beautiful'.[8] Rossiter, who followed, talked about the problems of having children in the Gallery, explaining that, although in principle he thought they should be allowed in, they sometimes had to be restrained from throwing objects at the works of art. The question of children in the Gallery was a recurring issue, and one of several where Rossiter (faced with the problems on the spot) and the Council (particularly the childless Watts) had to thrash out a compromise of some kind.

Even these profound difficulties might have been overcome, since both Leighton and Rossiter were, after all, working to the same end, but the foundation of the Gallery itself involved a major stumbling block. Rossiter had set up the Gallery, he had bought Portland House in his own name, and he himself lived in the house. An annual grant of £300 from the City Parochial Trustees was thrown into doubt because the trustees wanted to see the Gallery finances made properly accountable. Political issues were undoubtedly involved in attitudes towards the Gallery, and Rossiter was regarded by some (although not by Leighton) as a dangerous radical. As late as 1894, when the Gallery was already open, Leighton told Mary Watts that Sir Baldwyn Leighton 'has got hold of some story about Rossiter using the gallery for socialist Propaganda – "which is absurd" as Euclid says'.[9]

Meetings of the Council were sometimes held in Watts' home at Little Holland House and sometimes at the South London Art Gallery, but more often in Leighton's studio in Holland Park Road. With its casts of the Elgin marbles and rich furnishings, the room reflected the painter's own aspirations, but must have seemed a million miles from Peckham Road. Mary Watts commented with wry humour that her husband and Edward Burne-Jones, like the other Council members, attended most of the meetings. 'Perhaps neither of these two was ever seen at a meeting of any other Council.'[10] Such, it seems, was the power of Frederic Leighton's personality.

The meetings were sometimes stormy, particularly after the Council had decided to try to wrest ownership from Rossiter in 1893, a move which the Treasurer stoutly resisted. By that time, Georgiana Burne-Jones had become, after Leighton, the most important member of the Council. Like Leighton, Georgie MacDonald (as she then was) had grown up with principles of social duty, the result, in her case, of a Methodist upbringing. By the 1880s, she had untapped a well of organising ability and a strong social conscience, fuelled by her friendship with William Morris. When Leighton approached Burne-Jones for help with the South London Art Gallery, he readily agreed, but the unworldly painter was hardly a natural organiser or fund-raiser. It was Georgie who set about borrowing works from her husband's friends and associates and collecting money from his patrons, among them Percy Wyndham, whose name appears in one of the early donation lists.

Five letters written to John Cross, George Eliot's widower, in late September and October 1890

Lady Burne-Jones (photo by Frederick Hollyer).

express Georgie Burne-Jones's gratitude for his proposed gift in memory of his wife, and invite him to visit the half-completed Gallery with her. While her letters speak of 'we', she regularly says that her husband is unwell or away in Rottingdean, and it is clear that the impulse came from herself: 'We are thankful for the disposition of your heart to help our dear struggling Gallery – as we believe that anything given "in memory of George Eliot" will evoke more, for with many it is a name to conjure with.'[11]

Mary Watts arrived on the Council in a very similar way to Georgie Burne-Jones. Both were the active wives of painters without much gift for practical matters. From the evidence of Mary Watts' diary, however, Watts often discussed South London Art Gallery issues with her and seems to have

Mrs G. F. Watts (oil by G. F. Watts, Watts Gallery, Compton).

taken a real interest in the Gallery's affairs. Mary Watts had some of Leighton's idealism about the benefits of art. She had married a husband years older than herself, and felt that she was making a contribution to the highest form of painting by enabling him to work and by recording his every word. She was a talented artist herself, and after Watts' death designed and built the Mortuary Chapel at Compton in Surrey.

Although Leighton tended to think of Mary Watts and Georgie Burne-Jones as a team, and although they were clearly personally friendly, they approached the work of the Gallery from different standpoints, Georgie Burne-Jones's position being more politically radical. Leighton was thankful for the two women's contribution. In a letter to Mary Watts of 29 October 1892, he expressed gratitude 'for what you and Mrs B. Jones have done, you dear and capital Mary, in the Rossiter-Passmore business, of which I have heard thro' the little man [Rossiter]'.[12] Two months later, he was again thanking her warmly for 'your

and Signor's [Watts] truly kind suggestion about the children; on which I have made suggestions which I should like you both to see before final action is taken. He will I hope forward my letters, or their contents to you'.[13]

Mary Watts' diary for 1893 survives and gives a clear account of the course of events in that year. On 7 January she reported that 'we' (presumably the Council) 'send little Rossiter excellent paper on his work – the history of the Gallery, & the reasons for the existing order of things – very well set forth'.[14] Two weeks later, Leighton wrote to ask whether the Watts would support him at a meeting of the Charity Commissioners, but there is no account of the meeting.

By the time that Watts laid the foundation stone in March 1893, it was clear that the focus of the new institution had changed. One of the speakers, the Rev H. Percy Thompson, spoke of Passmore Edwards' gift of a library and a thousand volumes with somewhat tactless warmth, explaining that the Art Gallery had been something of an afterthought. The library, still the more important project, had recently been somewhat overlooked. What had happened, although Thompson did not say so, was that the effective members of the Council were painters or those committed to the visual arts.

Mary Watts meanwhile managed to interest Passmore Edwards in a project of her own, the Home Arts and Industries Association, with which she was much involved in the summer of 1893. In early July, however, her attention was drawn back to the South London Art Gallery. The Watts received a letter from Rossiter telling them that the City Parochial Trustees wanted to revise the trust and 'to alter his position & Miss Olver's from being life appointments – it seemed to us, something like a censure on them – & stirring up a feeling of resistance and counter demand in them. I am afraid this is the beginning of the end for the poor little people'.[15] Mary Watts was clearly torn, recognising that without William Rossiter and Mary Olver 'the Gallery will be better managed & be of more use'.[16] On his wife's instructions, Watts wrote to Leighton suggesting a meeting of the

Passmore Edwards (oil by G. F. Watts, N.P.G., London).

like expressing mistrust in them – he agreed, but says it ought never to have been & he opposed it at the very first. I said Mr Rossiter was not called in to do the work of the council, they were brought together by him. Yes he said but remember it is the council who have got him his gallery and his funds as they are now – it is the penalty of having called together such a powerful council'.[17]

Leighton, Mary Watts noticed, was 'courteousness itself' throughout the arduous work on the trust deed. 'To many of the members', she wrote later, 'it was a singular opportunity for seeing Sir Frederic's power of taking infinite pains with whatever work he might put his hand to; his self-control under trying circumstances, his tact and his resource.'[18] Leighton wrote to her, immediately after the meeting, expressing a hope that

'you and Mrs Ned felt that the best was done that could be done for our excellent but impossible little friend the Treasurer – I think, if you won't be angry with me for saying so, that in the great kindness of your hearts you both did not <u>quite</u> realize (to me an Americanism) that we were not dealing with ordinary matter for Council minutes or with any matter in which personal considerations could find <u>expression</u> but with a <u>formal businesslike Trust deed</u> defining, not for the moment but as a permanent charter, the conditions under which we, the Trust hold, are <u>responsible to the public for</u>, and must use for the public good certain monies and property vested in us'.[19]

What provoked this outburst of male condescension was probably not only Mary Watts' brief audience with the President, but Georgie Burne-Jones' speech at the meeting. As reported by Mary Watts: 'little Mrs Burne-Jones said a word or two to try & show the council's appreciation of Mr Rossiter's untiring and unselfish efforts'.[20] Georgie Burne-Jones was clearly more sympathetic to Rossiter than anyone else on the Council. In 1890 she had told John Cross: 'we are greatly interested in the Gallery & in Mr Rossiter – the story of it is a

Council without Rossiter and asking for a copy of the proposed changes to the trust deed.

The meeting, at which Rossiter *was* in fact present, took place on 16 July, Mary Watts and Georgie Burne-Jones having met beforehand to discuss their position. As the two hour meeting went on, Mary Watts took a decided dislike to Sir Raymond West, a former judge with the Indian Civil Service, and now, in his retirement, a reader in Indian Law at Cambridge. West's long association with education work had begun with his appointment as Vice Chancellor of Bombay University. To Mary Watts, however, West seemed prejudiced and illiberal, with

'a disagreeable feeling towards them both [Rossiter and Mary Olver], & sneers continually, which brings a look of pain across Sir Frederic's face – where strong feeling is expressed in the plainest way! He [Leighton] gave me a minute's audience, & I was able to say we felt the alteration of their position in the Trust deed <u>now</u>, seemed to us something romance'.[21] At one point, Burne-Jones wrote to Watts complaining that he saw nothing of his wife but the top of his head over a pile of letters, seven years of Rossiter's correspondence which she was trying to sort out.

Mary Watts' account of the meeting continues:

'[Rossiter] does not accept the Hon'ry Vice Presidentship with any grace – the more he believes that it [is] only meant as a salve to the soreness from the alteration of his permanent position – Strange little man. he has no sense of his own incapacity for the management of so large a thing he told us he could manage the National and British Museum tomorrow if he was anxious to do so!'[22]

This was Mary Watts' version. Leighton complained to her that Rossiter had no financial sense: 'My hair still stands on end when I remember the views about finance (and his own financial practice) which he quite innocently developed a short time back.'[23] Rossiter was delighted to be able to rent his house to the Council, rather than sell it to them, without, Leighton thought, 'seeing that so he is barred from selling or bequeathing it, it is no longer in effect his property, and what he has, viz. lifelong occupancy is exactly what he refused with such warmth'.[24] Leighton was hurt by Rossiter's reaction to the Vice President's proposal: 'I was very very sorely tried, inside, when he curtly and unhesitatingly flung back at us the one thing which it had been possible to do in the Trust deed to mark, and only to mark our sense of his great services – that was the acme of gracelessness!'

Leighton's aim was to pass the management of the Gallery to the local authority, and so place the establishment upon a more permanent footing. There remained the problem of Rossiter, still the treasurer and still living in Portland House. If Rossiter could be persuaded to resign from the Treasurership, Leighton wanted to replace him with James Pyke Thompson, 'our greatest benefactor'.[25] Pyke Thompson of Cardiff had presented the Gallery with a gift of one thousand pounds, and in 1891 was listed as the Gallery's Auditor.

Another attempt was made to buy Portland House in late 1894 when a meeting (without Rossiter) was held 'to consider . . . what offer we can make him'.[26] The Watts were now living in Surrey, and Leighton told Mary not to make the effort to attend: 'when the offer is formally made to him it will be well to have a full commit[tee]'.[27] A week later he forwarded her a letter:

'setting down exactly the terms we propose to offer to Mr Rossiter for his life interest – will you and Signor kindly let me know whether they have your assent'.[28]

A letter from Leighton to J. D. Linton sets out the position clearly:

'The time has come when it must be placed on a sound footing irrespective of personal feelings and susceptibilities . . . It is my intention & that of several others to offer to our friend Rossiter, worthy but obstinate man, the alternative of giving up the Treasurership as required by C[ity] P[arochial] T[rustees] or seeing us retire from the Council of the Gallery.'[29]

The struggle to wrest power from Rossiter did not entirely divert Leighton from the more positive issue of acquisitions. A few years before, he had been consulted on a similar subject by T. C. Horsfall, who was instrumental in setting up the Manchester Museum of Art. Horsfall asked Leighton to advise on the kind of collection which would be of true value to the city's inhabitants. Leighton suggested that Horsfall should not restrict himself to paintings, which might be of low quality. Prints and photographs of great architectural and sculptural works could be of more value. Leighton objected strongly, however, to commissioning copies: 'the overwhelming majority of even reasonable copies is to my mind worse than useless'.[30] He recommended hanging 'free, but faithful, coloured sketches of the picture' next to photographs, so that those who were unable to see the original works could understand the detail, the scheme and the colour.

On more than one occasion, Leighton insisted that Horsfall should not confine himself to works of art which were regarded as morally uplifting. He objected vigorously to the plan to exclude all works showing the nude from the Manchester Museum of Art and tried to dissuade Horsfall from commissioning works on specific subjects. In Leighton's view, such commissions inhibited an artist's natural talent. Horsfall's determination to refuse works which did not show a noble subject appalled Leighton, and he was equally unimpressed when G. F. Watts suggested, in a letter to the press, that the heroic deeds of the poor should be represented by paintings in public places, and so provide a source of inspiration to those who saw them. Walter Crane, who supported this plan, eventually worked with Emilie Barrington on a series of appropriate panels for Octavia Hill's Settlement in Red Cross Street, Southwark. Leighton, for his part, insisted that what mattered was high artistic quality, not improving subjects: 'The difficulty lies in the combination of the two objects which are quite independent of one another though not necessarily antagonistic.'[31]

Among the supporters of the Gallery movement were those who stressed the utilitarian advantages to be gained from stimulating a new generation of designers. Leighton, while granting the point, was not much interested in it, briefly telling Horsfall: 'The necessity on broad grounds of material national prosperity of developing whatever artistic gift may exist among us has been so often dwelt on that it should be needless to say more on it.'[32]

Leighton gave twelve engravings, eleven from his own paintings and one from Watts' portrait of himself. He lent one of two studies of a Roman model, both entitled *Vittoria* and executed in Ernest Hébert's studio in Rome in the 1870s.[33] Leighton painted numerous female heads and, from the evidence of a photograph, this was a good example. Nevertheless, *Vittoria*, like the *Street in Algiers* which Leighton also lent to the Gallery, was essentially a holiday work, and not regarded by the artist in the same light as his major Royal Academy pieces.

One additional loan from Leighton's private collection was a sketch for the famous Van Dyck *Children of Charles I*. This painting was not in the

Walter Crane (oil by G. F. Watts, N.P.G., London).

artist's sale, nor was it lent, as were many of his old masters, to the Royal Academy Winter Exhibition. As with the female head and the landscape, it seems likely that Leighton lent a less valued work to the South London Art Gallery.

One artist member of the Council who did not lend or donate a painting was J. D. Linton. Early in 1894, Linton threatened to resign his vice-presidentship, and Leighton, whose health was already beginning to fail, wrote to persuade him to change his mind:

'we fully understand that you may find difficulty in attending our meetings regularly – but this [is] by no means necessary & we shall be glad if you will attend when you conveniently can. Your co-operation & advice in Council have been of great use & your name is of value to the Institution.'[34]

Early in 1895, Leighton became ill with what was eventually diagnosed as angina. During this period, Linton took on some of the President's duties at the South London Art Gallery. As part of his move to re-organise the Gallery's finances, Leighton instructed Linton to hand over the accounts to Pyke Thompson for auditing by a professional accountant:

'under a small committee of the Trustees & two members to be nominated by me according to a certain schedule attached to our Trust deed. Lady Burne Jones, who has gone into these matters more closely than anyone, has consented to be one of them and I very much desire that you should be the other – it would involve only one meeting.'[35]

In mid-March, Leighton had to miss an important Council meeting for a doctor's appointment, and asked Linton to stand in, telling him that the Trust and schedule had been left out in case they were needed. His exasperation is clear in his complaint that Rossiter's wish to give up his position while asking the committee to retain 'a mental reservation' about it 'is a piece of sharp practice – a fraud in fact – as for the book money it must either be used by us for the purpose to which it was destined or returned to the donor':[36]

'Meanwhile I strongly take the view that the future prosperity . . . of our gallery depends on R's resigning all but the trusteeship and selling the house right out – without this all is wasted time and labour & some of us would find the solution – perhaps all – in leaving him & his house to himself and withdrawing altogether – He will then be free – and afterwards? Well that is his affair.'[37]

During the spring of 1895, Leighton, on the jury selecting works for the Academy exhibition, effectively handed over the South London Art Gallery business to Linton, but retained a sharp interest in events. On 11 April, however, Leighton gave up the struggle to work as usual, and went abroad, hoping to regain his health in a warmer climate. He returned in June, unrestored, and did not effectively take up his South London Art Gallery office again. In November he heard from Wyke Bayliss that the 'Gordian knot' of the South London Art Gallery had 'been at last unravelled'.[38]

Georgie Burne-Jones and Bayliss, with a financial adviser but without Linton, had negotiated the handing over of the Gallery to the Libraries Division of the Camberwell Vestry: 'I cannot tell you what trouble it has taken to transfer the whole thing to public control and establish it – but it is done at last', she wrote in 1897, when the final steps had been taken.[39] The task of putting on exhibitions also fell upon Georgie Burne-Jones' shoulders. As her biographer puts it:

'with meticulous attention to detail, Georgie personally undertook much of the organisation, including the mundane but necessary task of collecting the works, arranging the insurance cover and getting pictures suitably framed.'[40]

Leighton died in January 1896, having just been raised to the peerage. The struggle with Rossiter was not only the problem of Leighton's last years. He was also locked in a frustrating battle with St. Paul's Cathedral who were blocking his attempt to have Alfred Stevens' memorial to the Duke of Wellington erected. Rossiter was, however, a cause of acute stress to him. 'You have no idea what an interminable (and irritating) correspondence I have had with that terrible little man', Leighton told G. F. Watts.[41] After the two hour meeting of July 1893, he complained to Mary Watts: 'I was so wearied with trying to be amiable and yet standing firm where need was that I was unfit for my Richter Concert (the last and I have been to none) and had to give it up.'[42] It is probable that the Rossiter problem had helped to weaken Leighton's heart and so bring about his premature death.

On 6 January 1898, Leighton's successor as President of the Royal Academy, Edward Poynter, formally opened the new Art School complex. As Georgiana Burne-Jones' brother-in-law, Poynter had been unable to refuse, although he was very unenthusiastic about the task. In his speech, he declared that:

'it was a matter of rejoicing that the building should, at the suggestion of the donor [Passmore Edwards], be dedicated to the memory of Lord Leighton, who stood so high amongst

English painters, as an artist in the real sense of the word, and as one having a complete mastery of his craft, as opposed to that fatal amateur element which was so frequently seen in our artists and craftsmen.'[43]

Poynter went to talk about the fatal effect of dilettantism and empty enthusiasm. What was needed, he insisted, was 'fine craftsmen who would put their best work into all they did for the love of it'.[44] In conclusion, Poynter managed to work in a favourable reference to Leighton, whom he had much admired, while still retaining his hectoring stance: 'The name of Lord Leighton ought to be an incentive to use the Camberwell Institution in the only direction in which it could be of real value.'[45]

What Leighton would have thought of the proceedings is by no means clear. Burne-Jones was outraged by Poynter's 'materialist emphasis'. The speech, he believed, had not 'cast a chill over the proceedings – he literally scattered dust and ashes of death and the charnel house on them. I think it must have been that he was in a fury at having to go there at all. Said nothing to smarten anyone up – seemed almost ashamed of being an artist'.[46] Poynter himself was 'so cross . . . he said he'd never go to such a thing again'. But a farcical element hung around the end of that opening day. Philip Burne-Jones tried to cheer Poynter up by taking him to a favourite restaurant, but, on emerging, as Philip later told his father, 'he was pursued into his vehicle by two Regent Street ladies. I should have thought they wouldn't have gone after a man of his age'.[47]

FOOTNOTES

1. Letter to Mrs. Benson, 23 April 1894, Royal Academy.
2. E. Barrington, *Leighton and John Kyrle*, 1903, p.17.
3. ibid, p.16.
4. The catalogue entries refer to M. A. Darbishire, presumably a mistake for H. A.
5. M. Watts, *George Frederic Watts*, 1912, II, 229.
6. ibid.
7. E. Russell Barrington, *The Life of Lord Leighton*, 1906, II, 8.
8. S. L. A. G., 1890.
9. Letter to Mary Watts, 24 January 1894, Royal Borough of Kensington and Chelsea Libraries, 12791.
10. Watts, 1912.
11. Letter of 12 October 1890, Southwark Record Office.
12. Letter of 29 October 1892, Kensington and Chelsea Libraries, 12775.
13. Letter of 21 December 1892, Kensington and Chelsea Libraries.
14. Mary Watts, entry for 7 January 1893, manuscript diary, Watts Gallery, Compton. I am indebted to the Chairman of the Watts Gallery Trustees and to Richard Jeffries, Curator of the Watts Gallery.
15. ibid, 10 July 1893.
16. ibid.
17. ibid.
18. Watts, 1912.
19. Letter of 10 July 1893, Kensington and Chelsea Libraries, 12777.
20. Mary Watts, diary, 10 July 1893.
21. Letter of 26 September 1890, Southwark Record Office.
22. Mary Watts, diary, 10 July 1893.
23. Letter of 10 July 1893, Kensington and Chelsea Libraries, 12777.
24. ibid.
25. Letter of 19 December 1894, Kensington and Chelsea Libraries, 12799.
26. Letter of 12 December 1894, Kensington and Chelsea Libraries, 12798.
27. ibid.
28. Letter of 19 December 1894, Kensington and Chelsea Libraries, 12799.
29. Letter of 21 November 1894, Beinecke Library, Yale. I am very grateful to the Beinecke Library for the use of these references.
30. Russell Barrington, 1906, II, 277.
31. Alice Corkran, *Frederic Leighton*, 1904, p.157.
32. Letter of 21 March 1889, Manchester City Art Gallery.
33. One version of *Vittoria* was shown at the Royal Society of British Artists in 1873, but did not sell, and both versions were still in the artist's possession at the time of his death. See L. and R. Ormond, 1975, cat. no. 213-4.
34. Letter of 27 February 1894, Beinecke Library.
35. ibid.
36. Letter to Linton of 18 March 1895, Beinecke Library.
37. ibid.
38. Letter to Linton of 27 November 1895, Beinecke Library.
39. Ina Taylor, *Victorian Sisters*, 1987, pp.156-7.
40. Letter of 19 December 1894, Kensington and Chelsea Libraries, 12799.
41. ibid.
42. Letter of 10 July 1893, Kensington and Chelsea Libraries, 12777.
43. J. Passmore Edwards, *A Few Footprints*, 1905, p.67.
44. ibid, p.68.
45. ibid.
46. Thomas Rooke, *Burne-Jones Talking*, ed. Mary Lago, 1981, p.167.
47. ibid, p.166.

'In the Picture Gallery'.

Giles Waterfield

Art for the People

The history of the South London Art Gallery offers a microcosm of the complex development of the public provision of art and culture in late nineteenth century Britain. This essay aims to relate the Gallery to the expansion of cultural provision in late Victorian Britain; to consider the growth of the idea of museums intended for the population of poor areas of great cities; and to examine the pattern of patronage which produced this Gallery. The surviving collection at Camberwell offers a revealing, if not always lucid, insight into the execution of a project to which the modern observer may react with hesitation, but which stimulates enquiry into the political and social role of an artistic institution intended for the working man and woman.

The South London Art Gallery should be seen in the context of a group of museums and galleries set up with an educational purpose in the poorer areas of great cities in the late nineteenth century. The most notable of these were the Manchester Art Museum or the Ancoats or Horsfall Museum, as it was variously called, devised in the late 1870s and established at Ancoats Hall in 1886; the art exhibitions organised from 1881 at St. Jude's National School in Whitechapel in East London, until the erection of a permanent building in the Whitechapel Art Gallery; the Ruskin museum near Sheffield, at Walkley (1878), moved to Meersbrook in 1890; and the South London Art Gallery. Though close to contemporary art museums in their collections, in their didactic intentions, in their approach to display, and in the freedom of access that they allowed the public, these enterprises were exceptional. They were intended primarily for working people, being sited (apart from the Ruskin museum) in depressed urban areas, and shared the aim of introducing the

power of art to the local population, bringing into what were perceived as their joyless lives an intimation of a happier existence.

Though each establishment depended on an individual group of supporters, there was a considerable degree of cohesion between the various initiatives. Many of the artists who gave or lent their pictures to the Whitechapel were also involved with the South London Art Gallery. Equally, the organisers regularly consulted one another, the Ancoats Museum and its educational activities being regarded as a particular source of inspiration. At the same time, these galleries and museums should be related to a much wider social initiative in late Victorian Britain: the efforts by representatives of the upper and middle classes to organise the leisure of the working class population by offering educational, cultural and sporting opportunities.[1] Frequently such activities were provided by 'settlements' or 'missions', close in inspiration and style to colonial enterprises. Walter Besant's tone in writing about the East End is characteristic of the sense purveyed by those involved of venturing into the unknown: he wrote of 'the far East, in that region of London which is less known to Englishmen than if it were situated in the wildest part of Colorado, or among the pine forests of British Columbia'.[2] These endeavours involved the creation of communities in deprived areas in which middle class representatives of universities, men or women, and usually young, would settle, devoting the whole or part of their time to this generally (but not always) secular ministry. These settlements were closely related to the idea of the 'philanthropic' gallery: the Barnetts set up Toynbee Hall, a developed example of the type, with the intention of creating the nucleus of a university of East London, in 1884, while from 1891

Great Ancoats Street, Manchester, c.1900.

A slum in the East End, used in lantern slide lectures by Henrietta Barnett.

LIFE AND LABOUR

OF THE

PEOPLE IN LONDON

BY

CHARLES BOOTH

ASSISTED BY

JESSE ARGYLE,   ERNEST AVES,   GEO. E. ARKELL
ARTHUR L. BAXTER,   GEORGE H. DUCKWORTH

Third Series: Religious Influences

OUTER SOUTH LONDON

London
MACMILLAN AND CO., LIMITED
NEW YORK: THE MACMILLAN CO.
1902

Ancoats Hall accommodated not only the museum but a University Settlement, more modest than Toynbee Hall but comparable in its aims.

These 'philanthropic' galleries have stimulated much recent interest. It is not the purpose of this essay to recapitulate the excellent studies, by Frances Borzello of the Whitechapel Art Gallery[3] and by Michael Harrison of the Ancoats Museum,[4] but rather to consider the character of these enterprises in relation to the South London Art Gallery. These endeavours to stimulate artistic activity in deprived areas have a strange resonance for the modern observer, for whom the remoteness of late Victorian society cannot prevent reminders of contemporary urban life, and for whom questions of social engineering, of the manipulation of the population by those exercising political and cultural power, remain as vital now as they were a century ago.

* * *

The last three decades of the nineteenth century witnessed a powerful reaction against social conditions in the great industrial cities among an influential sector of the British population. It was a reaction which in literary terms was to be expressed both in such popular publications as Walter Besant's *All Sorts and Conditions of Men*, of 1882, and in the extended survey of housing and living conditions in London carried out by Charles Booth from 1885 to 1902: *Life and Labour of the People in London*. In visual terms, the most notable expressions of the same fascinated horror were

Gustave Doré's drawings of London, and the social realist paintings of Frank Holl, Hubert von Herkomer and Luke Fildes, executed from the 1870s onwards. The deprivation and squalor depicted in these works aroused public outcry, some of which was expressed in short term efforts to deal with the problems: but more sustained attempts were also made to improve the quality of life of the inhabitants of great cities, by replacing the stock of housing in town centres and by building cities of a new sort. Much of this effort, on the traditional English pattern which distrusted organised activity in the social field by the state, was due to private endeavour, but the increasing effectiveness of local government both in the capital and in provincial centres was able to make a more decisive contribution.

By the 1870s municipal government had generally dealt with the most pressing problems (of, for example, sanitation) that it had faced in its earliest days, and was developing a comprehensive machinery of government, reflected in its ambitious town halls. Equally, the archaic system of local government in the capital was reshaped by the creation of the London County Council in 1888 and its empowerment under the Housing of the Working Class Act to address the problem of slum housing. A vigorous attempt to create a decent, if plain, standard of workers' accommodation in the capital was made by the Council's Architects' Department (many of whose members were disciples of Webb and Lethaby, close in their beliefs to the central figures of the South London Art Gallery). Conventional expectations of urban settlements were undermined by the Garden City Movement, which had been initiated by the publications of Ebenezer Howard at the end of the nineteenth century, and by the laying out of Letchworth Garden City. The Garden City encouraged the idea of the educational museum as a centre of cultural and social life, expressed, for example, by the educational and social reformer Patrick Geddes in *City Development: A Study of Parks, Gardens and Culture-Institutes*, of 1904, in which he proposed an ideal semi-urban community containing an art museum, a music hall (of an improv-

E. A. Waterlow, *Early Morning in the Thames Valley* (No. 61).

ing nature) and educational botanical gardens. Henrietta Barnett, to whom the exhibitions at the Whitechapel Art Gallery were largely due, devoted much of her life from 1907 to the creation of Hampstead Garden Suburb, which was intended not only to recreate village life close to the centre of London, but to engage in social engineering on the lines already explored at Whitechapel, by juxtaposing in one community middle class and artisan housing. At Camberwell, the new Gallery was seen as providing a social and educational focus in a characterless and monotonous stretch of the capital.

The later nineteenth century witnessed a powerful movement to improve facilities for the urban poor. These efforts, again, generally emanated from private initiatives but were taken up by local government. Amenities which had come to be regarded as essential extended from public baths to parks. The interest in the provision of open spaces extended to the preservation of common land and of historic buildings, illustrated most forcefully by the work of Commons Preservation Society, by the establishment of the Society for the Protection of Ancient Buildings, and by the foundation of the National Trust in 1895. Many of the leading figures in these movements played an important part in the creation of opportunities for

Drawing class, Myrdle Street School, 1908.

the working class, and particularly in the work of the South London Art Gallery.

* * *

In comparison with other European nations, Britain was hesitant to introduce universal education, partly from fear of interference by the state. The Education Act of 1870, which introduced school boards, still did not enforce a universal system, although it made the creation of such a system possible. The years between 1870 and the outbreak of the First World War nevertheless witnessed a major expansion of schools in Britain, compulsory universal education finally being introduced in 1902.

The movement for adult education, especially for workers, had grown steadily since the 1820s. The Mechanics' Institutes founded in the 1820s and later, especially in London and the North around Leeds and Manchester, offered, for very modest subscriptions, libraries, lectures and exhibitions. These were ostensibly aimed at manual workers, though the actual users tended, by a process that was to be common during the century, to be a more prosperous sector of the community, such as skilled craftsmen and clerks. The London Working Men's College, founded by F. D. Maurice in 1854, attempted to offer higher education to a working class audience which would otherwise have been excluded from such opportunities, on the understanding that intellect was not the privilege of the wealthy. It was from this long but essentially voluntary and only intermittently successful tradition that the first impetus for the South London Working Men's College (as the precursor of the Gallery was styled) derived.

Essentially allied to the organisation of adult education was the provision of public libraries by local boroughs, first permitted by the Museum and Libraries Act of 1850. By the end of the century an effective free library service was available in most towns, though it was often private money which paid for the actual construction of buildings. Again, the South London Art Gallery owed its inspiration to the belief that libraries should be provided in every centre of population: in its early days the library service was of greater importance than the exhibitions.

* * *

The growth of general education gave a major impetus to museums, especially museums of art. In 1870 these were restricted to the National Galleries in London and Edinburgh, and a small group of university galleries and private institutions. Only the most tentative efforts had been made, in the late 1850s and the 1860s, to set up municipal art collections. By 1914 every English and Scottish town of any consequence boasted a municipal art gallery, or at least a façade behind which art could be exhibited.

The earliest municipal galleries, as set up in Birmingham in 1867 and Nottingham in 1878, depended on the idea of the craft museum. They often opened without permanent collections, relying on temporary exhibitions of paintings by local artists or loans from South Kensington of instructive examples of metalwork or engravings. A little later, in the late 1880s, a further type of art museum developed, based on a personal collection, such as the Mappin Art Gallery in Sheffield of 1887. These reflected a period when the visual arts reached a new level of esteem and artists a new level of wealth, and when the symbolic leader of the profession, Leighton, was admitted to the peerage, the first time such an honour had been extended to a painter. The dual purpose of these museums – as educational craft collections and as displays of cultural capital in its most flamboyant form – led to an ambiguous relationship in their collections between the fine and decorative arts, one which was to be reflected at the South London Art Gallery. The new art museums were extremely popular: Birmingham Museum and Art Gallery (with its associated Aston Hall) received 1,300,000 visitors in 1886 at a time when the population of the city was under 500,000, while the Leeds City Art Gallery regularly counted over a quarter of a million visitors in the 1890s (out of a population of 367,000), rising to 420,000 in 1898. Such success depended heavily on temporary exhibitions, a crucial feature of these museums. The visitors to these new museums appear to have been drawn from the whole population, excepting only the poorest members of society.

The collections in these new museums depended primarily on gifts and bequests, and to a much lesser extent on purchases made from the Royal Academy or from the museum's annual exhibition of contemporary artists' work. Reflecting the taste of local magnates, they tended to concentrate on contemporary British work. They stressed local links, with views of the patronal town and its scenery as an important element, and with a strong representation of artists born or practising in the locality. Though works by academic foreign artists were included, no interest was shown in the contemporary initiatives being made on the Continent, while a shortage of funds prevented more than a perfunctory representation of paintings before 1800, unless as the result of a donation or bequest. Such was very much the pattern of the Camberwell collection.

The values espoused by these new institutions were those of established bourgeois culture: a generally declining aristocracy played no part in their formation, any more than did the working class. At a time when civic display in the great cities was reaching its highest point, the city museum and gallery tended to be situated in the municipal centre, as at Birmingham, Leeds or Liverpool, in a more or less imposing building, often adjacent and symbolically subsidiary to the town hall, serving as an element of the structure of metropolitan power, with the espousal of traditional values expressed by the almost universal choice of classical architecture, at least for façade and entrance hall.

While the museums of the late nineteenth century recognised the convention that such institutions contributed to what was conceived of as the fabric of civilised urban living, their intimate relationship with existing structures of power made them less than ideal in the view of many reformers. The councils and curators responsible for these institutions showed on the whole little interest in innovative educational ideas. It was a role that was to be explored much more actively by the 'philanthropic' galleries.

*   *   *

The South London Art Gallery always prided itself on its accessibility: open on Sundays ('This is the only Collection of Art Works in all London that is open on Sunday' proclaimed the Gallery's *Weekly Notes*), open in the evenings, positively welcoming to children. In this respect it represented the culmination, though a very specific culmination, limited to a working class educational museum, of a long transition from the private to the public institution. Of its nature the museum must raise questions about the relationship between objects on display and their audience. The fundamental motives for the creation of museums – the collection, preservation, categorisation and display of specimens of material culture – prompt enquiry over the purpose of these activities, positing the existence of an audience and questioning the extent to which such an audience can be restricted. The relationship between the museum collection – initially undertaken by private individuals, whether aristocrats or scholars, for a polite and learned audience, for the eighteenth-century definition of 'public' – and the

This is the only Collection of Art Works in all London that is open on Sundays.

SOUTH LONDON FINE ART GALLERY
AND
FREE LIBRARY,
207, CAMBERWELL ROAD.

Established 1868.

The Art Gallery is open every day, except Saturdays, from 3.30 to 5.30 & 7 to 9.30 p.m.

The Library is open every evening, 7 to 9.30.

PUBLIC BUILDINGS IN LONDON.

NORTH OF THE THAMES.	SOUTH OF THE RIVER.
MUSEUMS.	
British.	
South Kensington.	None.
Natural History.	
&c., &c., &c.	
ART GALLERIES.	
National Gallery.	
South Kensington.	
Royal Academy.	None.
Society of British Artists.	
Water Color Galleries.	
&c., &c., &c.	
LIBRARIES.	
British Museum.	
South Kensington.	None.
Guildhall.	
&c., &c., &c.	

The Free Libraries Act has been adopted in every Parish in or near which we have been working, and in few others in London.

Annual Report, 1888.

broader public (in the modern sense of the whole population) developed from the late eighteenth century onwards. Although the Ashmolean Museum was available to all from the time it was established in 1683, the trustees of the British Museum (which opened in 1759) made the visitor, for many years, as unwelcome as possible. By contrast, at the National Gallery, founded in 1824, it was the wish of Prime Minister and trustees that the new institution should be as readily visited as any contemporary museum on the Continent: it was to be free to the public except on the two days a week that it was reserved for artists, and open to children (this was an issue that was to be much debated during the century) to allow their parents to visit. From its earliest days the National Gallery was mobbed by visitors, especially after the move to Trafalgar Square in 1838: 500,000 were recorded in 1841, though the Gallery was only open four days a week and not at all at weekends.[5] The central location of the Gallery was regarded as of crucial importance. The same principle was jealously defended thirty years later when the Parliamentary Select Committee of 1853 on the National Gallery, alarmed by the effect of the noxious physical conditions in central London on the nation's paintings, investigated a move to the cleaner air of South Kensington. Although a number of witnesses advocated the move, the majority opposed it, on the grounds that such a change would debar many of the population, especially from East London, from visiting their national collection. With the rapid expansion of London to east and south, the location of the National Gallery in Trafalgar Square was less convenient: instead of being located at the heart of the ordinary city, the Gallery's site became the heart of the West End, psychologically remote from working people in East or South London.

In reaction to these changes, an influential body of the arts administrators associated with South Kensington, led by Henry Cole, envisaged a new form of museum. From its earliest days, the Museum of Manufactures or the South Kensington Museum as it became in 1857 was intended by the Department of Science and Art to offer an educative experience to its visitors, who were seen primarily as artisans. This was not, initially, to be a museum of fine works of art, but a teaching museum, instilling in the artisan-visitor an understanding of the finest qualities of design. The administrators of the Museum, under the superintendance of Cole, aimed to 'make the mode of admission as acceptable as possible to all classes of visitor'.[6] The Museum was to be open in the evening, this being the first time that such arrangements had been made in a public museum in Britain, so that workers who could otherwise not visit (the museum being closed on Sunday) should have the opportunity to do so. In the radical words of the Annual Report, 'It would appear to be less for the rich that the State should provide public galleries of paintings and objects of art and science, than for those classes who would be absolutely destitute of the enjoyment of them unless they were provided by the State'.[7] This experiment succeeded: in 1857 the number of visitors, assessed in proportion to the hours of opening, was five times greater in the evening (at 227,374 over the year) than during the day. Though the museum offered a jumble of collections, its educational purpose was supported by descriptive labelling (over which much care was taken), cheap catalogues, and public lectures, at which blocks of seats were reserved for working men. The South Kensington Museum played a crucial role in the development of museums and galleries through its encouragement of trade museums suitable for the aspiring craftsman and through its loans of reproductions and products considered to be of high quality. A number of the people most involved with its work – Leighton, Crane, Morris, for example – were to reappear at the South London Art Gallery.

Accessibility was to be a prime motive in the establishment of the new museums in deprived urban areas. London was in the peculiar position that whereas relatively small towns were, by the 1860s, frequently endowed with natural history or archaeology museums, the number and quality of national institutions in the capital inhibited the development of local collections, a situation not

Interior of Bethnal Green Museum.

helped by the slowness with which an adequate local government system was set up in London. Thus large and growing areas outside Westminster and Kensington possessed no cultural provision at all. In its 1865 Annual Report, the Secretary of the South Kensington Museum recorded that in July of the previous year the Lords of the Committee of the Council on Education had heard the 'prospectus of an East London Museum, issued 1859, . . . respecting the establishment of a South London Museum . . . also . . . a North London Museum', and had expressed their support for the establishment of 'two suburban galleries for Science and Art in the north-east and the south-east parts of London'.[8] The following year the Commissioners

on Education considered a scheme for the establishment of museums, illustrating branches of science, to be set up 'on behalf of the million artizans inhabiting the densely populated manufacturing and labouring districts in the east of London'.[9] As a result of this agitation, a museum was indeed established in the East End.

The museum which opened at Bethnal Green in 1872 in the discarded iron and glass sheds known as the Brompton Boilers represented the first and almost the last attempt by the state to provide a museum in a socially deprived area. Bethnal Green epitomised the reactive unplanned style in which the national museum system, if it can be so described, has come into existence in Britain.

Characteristically, the function and the scope of the Bethnal Green Museum were never defined until, after World War II, it was entitled the Museum of Childhood. Originally intended by Cole to allow the transfer of the South Kensington Museum's unwanted temporary buildings to East London, where the local inhabitants would be able to organise their own activities, it became instead a nationally-funded institution in which were deposited assorted unwanted exhibits from South Kensington, such as the Food Collection and the Museum of Economic Entomology, supplemented by temporary exhibitions of a type unrelated to the permanent displays or to the life of the local area (though the Food Collection was scarcely permanent, requiring regular restocking by courtesy of Fortnum and Mason). These temporary exhibitions, often drawn from private collections, were initiated at the opening in 1872 by the loan of paintings and furniture and objets d'art from the holdings of Sir Richard Wallace. According to contemporary accounts, the furniture, in particular, was eagerly studied by the local craftsmen (Bethnal Green is at the centre of the traditional furniture-making area) and could be seen as fulfilling temporarily the frequently discussed objective of a trade museum; but many of the exhibitions, such as that of Dulwich College Picture Gallery paintings lent in 1876 or Lord Bute's collection, appear to have been organised on the basis of what was currently available, with little thought given to their appropriateness to the purpose.[10] The Bethnal Green Museum was, certainly, hugely popular, with 25,557 visitors on its first day, and over 900,000 in the first year. Following Cole's practice at South Kensington, the hours were adapted to make it as accessible as possible, with evening openings until ten p.m. on three days a week and numerous free days (nobody went on the paying days, which were soon abandoned). In terms of a defined role, however, the disparate collections on display, the absence of any reflection of the character of the local area and the tendency of the South Kensington authorities to use it as a place of deposit, gave Bethnal Green the character of an ill-organised outpost of cultural colonialism,

presenting 'a jumbled and puzzling impression to the public'.[11] In this respect, it contrasted strongly with the highly directed character of, for example, the Manchester Art Museum.

The Bethnal Green display would not have appealed to the man who played a major part in defining the objectives of the 'working class museum': John Ruskin. Within the discourse over the role of the arts in society enunciated by Pugin, Arnold and Morris, Ruskin's views were of particular importance for the development of provision for the underprivileged. His ideas were of fundamental importance for the three major institutions intended to bring art to the people in late nineteenth-century London. He was the prime mentor for T. C. Horsfall in Manchester and hailed Horsfall's manifesto in the July 1877 edition of *Fors Clavigera*; and mottoes from his writings were used repeatedly in the Whitechapel exhibition catalogues.[12] At the South London Art Gallery the principal room was named after him, while a quotation from his writings inspired the Gallery's decorative symbol. For Ruskin, art held a position of central importance in life; it was not to be regarded as an ornament but as a force of quasi-religious strength, revealing divine attributes in visible form. In a world which, in Ruskin's view, was being degraded and destroyed by the forces of the industrial revolution, art offered a chance of redemption. A true understanding of art required protracted study: only by diligent looking, and copying, could a person hope to comprehend natural things, and the finest works of art. Ruskin stressed that a healthy society would be expressed in the nature of its art and architecture, a corrupt or enfeebled art (such as he perceived around him in Victorian Britain) mirroring a damaged society. These issues were seldom tackled with such vigour. In particular he addressed the question of the relationship between an under-educated proletariat and 'High Art', that is the artefacts of a past society using a system of cultural values far removed from the experience of nineteenth-century urban Britain. In the discussion of Select Committees in the 1830s and later, one of the frequently urged benefits of a National Gallery was that such an institution would improve the qualities of design among manufacturers and artisans – although no indication was given of how an understanding of design, applicable to the construction and decoration of contemporary furniture and ceramics, could be conveyed by a study of Old Master paintings and furniture. For Ruskin, the supposed value of Old Masters for artisans was specious. He did not believe that Renaissance painting could be appreciated by every visitor to a museum, since before it could be understood, the viewer's eye must be educated. The nation ought to provide art museums of two distinct types:

> 'A national museum is one thing, a national place of education another; and the more sternly and unequivocally they are separated the better will each perform its office – the one of treasuring, and the other of teaching.'[13]

Ruskin had a clear conception of the 'noble Museum of the best art' which would house the nation's artistic treasures,[14] even though, as he admitted, his ideas on what it should contain shifted. It was to be 'a stately place – a true Palace of Art, pure in the style of it indeed, and, as far as thought can reach, removed from grossness or excess of ornament . . . especially precious in material and exquisite in workmanship . . .'[15] For London he envisaged a building beside the Thames of three storeys containing sculpture on the lowest floor, the libraries and print rooms above and the pictures on the top storey. Externally it was to be of regular design comparable to the internal elevation of a cathedral, and built or inlaid with beautiful coloured stone or marble. Into this palace, where paintings would not be shown for architectural effect in picturesque masses on the walls but at eye-level in pleasing but not ostentatious rooms, only a select public would be admitted. He objected to the use of museums by inappropriate persons: 'You must not make your Museum a refuge against either rain or ennui, nor let into perfectly well-furnished, and even, in the true sense, palatial, rooms, the utterly squalid and ill-bred portion of the people.'[16] For such people,

Interior of the wooden extension of the museum at Walkley, 1884.

alternative refuges should be provided. As an active teacher of art at the Working Men's College in the 1850s, he felt that students should learn their skills by studying detail, by looking at true work, even if 'works not altogether the best',[17] and by copying casts, photographs and drawings and botanical specimens and minerals. Only at an advanced level would they study the greatest masterpieces.

The specific contribution made by Ruskin to the development of the workers' museum lay in his proposal that educational museums should be set up in every quarter of large cities. It was a theme to which he repeatedly returned, varying his emphasis as was his habit. But, essentially, these museums were to fulfil two major functions, epitomised by the museum he set up at Walkley. Firstly, they were intended as highly-ordered repositories for objects that could be used for copying by students: he developed these ideas when setting up the art school in the Ashmolean Museum. Secondly, educational museums, whether of art, or of natural history (the two could be presented together, or apart), were intended for the whole population and were to be organised with no less care than the national treasury. He was critical of the South Kensington Museum, filled as it was with fine things shown confusedly beside objects of poor quality, a confusion from which no educational meaning derived. He hoped for the creation of a 'large educational museum in every district of London, freely open every day, and well lighted and well warmed at night, with all furniture of comfort, and full aids for the use of their contents by all classes'.[18] These museums would in themselves serve as models of 'perfect order and perfect elegance' for 'the disorderly and rude populace',[19] who would be inspired to introduce similar qualities into their own houses. In these institutions would be displayed collections appropriate for the expected audience: 'A Museum, primarily, is to be for *simple* persons. Children, that is to say, and peasants . . . The Town Museum is to be for the Town's People, the Village Museum for the Villagers.' And for 'these simple people', the objects on view would manifest 'the beauty and life of all things and creatures in their perfectness'.[20] He suggested that an equivalent hierarchy of natural history displays should also be created, with the collections of the British Museum (the Natural History Museum had not become an independent entity at the time he wrote) serving as a national treasury, and with numbers of local institutions, arranged with the order and elegance appropriate to works of art. Such collections were set up, examples surviving at the Haslemere Educational Museum, founded in 1895 by a local philanthropist, Sir Jonathan Hutchinson, to illustrate the History of the Earth and of Man; and at Cawthorne near Barnsley in West Yorkshire, where the Cawthorne Victoria Jubilee Museum opened in 1884 with collections of birds and butterflies, minerals and antiquities, given in great part by Ruskin for this purpose to the Stanhope family.[21] This was indeed a Village Museum, filled

Interior of the Victoria Jubilee Museum, Cawthorne.

with objects of local interest, for the enjoyment and instruction of the local population. It survives in the half-timbered building designed for it by its benefactor, still conveying the character of a Ruskinian village museum.

T. C. Horsfall, as his various writings illustrate, intended his museum to function along lines comparable to those advocated by Ruskin. At the Ancoats Museum looking at pictures was seen as a morally improving activity, one that would bring out the best feelings in the spectator, for whom a painting of everyday life, if properly explained, could preach a sermon. The Museum was intended to provide 'the largest and most carefully-planned system which has yet been tried in a large town, for giving the mass of the people knowledge and admiration of nature and of the most useful and interesting forms of human work'.[22] Horsfall's museum, with its modern reproductions of old Delftware and Pompeian bronze ornaments, its contemporary drawings of scenery and old buildings, its photographs and copies of famous paintings and sculpture,[23] would convey practical insight into the artist's technique and give an understanding of the history of art, but would not be able, as Leighton urged it should, to convey a more idealistic appreciation of aesthetic experience. In most cases, paintings were treated as morally instructive illustrations,

Ancoats Hall, 1964.

The Staircase Hall, Ancoats Museum.

The Bird Room, Ancoats Museum.

The Children's Theatre, Ancoats Museum.

intended for example to give an understanding of the best thoughts and feelings of gifted people. The Museum was divided by subject matter, with rooms devoted variously to landscapes, foreign scenery, trees and wild flowers.[24] A model workers' room, provided by Morris, suggested how workers might furnish their own homes in a more tasteful and seemly way than was usual – if only they could afford the furnishings, since these turned out to be prohibitively expensive for most. Perhaps the most important exhibit in relation to the later development of museums was the Mothers' Room. Intended for children rather than their parents, this contained depictions of children by or after Murillo and Ford Madox Brown and Mrs Allingham, with cheerful illustrations of nursery tales by Walter Crane and Randolph Caldecott. The visual education of the young was of especial importance at Ancoats. Through the experience of these rooms, designed very much on the lines advocated by Ruskin, working people were to be taught to love the countryside, as well as to grasp such important concepts as the Aryan link between ancient Greece and modern England.[25] In addition, displays of beauty would not only bring cheer to people condemned to live in monotonous and ugly urban conditions, but would encourage such people to organise their lives so as to create beauty and order for themselves. From the point of view of the privileged classes, the creation of such an institution as the Manchester Art Museum would give those suffering from boredom and guilt the pleasant relief of sharing their knowledge and taste with those less fortunate than themselves.[26]

What gives an edge to the study of these institutions is the ambiguity of motivation in some of those most deeply involved, and in the character of very different enterprises. Though Horsfall's desire to provide sermons through pictures reflects a crude understanding of aesthetic experience, the Museum achieved a fair success with the local population, especially through its work with children. It is hard not to admire the determination with which in spite of frequent rebuffs he pursued enlightened members of the aristocracy, literary figures such as Tennyson and Matthew Arnold, painters including Leighton, Watts, Crane, Holman Hunt and, a generation later, William Rothenstein, art historians such as Sidney Cockerell and Sidney Colvin, professors of archaeology and Egyptology such as Sir Charles Newton and Flanders Petrie, with requests to speak at or advise on the collections of his museum, from the 1870s until close to his death in 1932.[27] And though Horsfall's objectives were to be rejected in the end by William Morris, for many years they attracted the support not only of Morris but of such radical socialists as Walter Crane and Charles Rowley. Rowley, a Manchester publisher, and an Ancoats man, devoted much energy and money to the Ancoats project; for him, more clearly perhaps than for Horsfall, one of the purposes of the Museum was to break down the barriers between social classes and to use the Museum as part of a much more extensive campaign of social transformation.

Equally, it is difficult for the modern historian to arrive at a fair assessment of the role of the Barnetts in Whitechapel. When Samuel and Henrietta Barnett moved to what their bishop described as the worst parish in London, they undertook what was to become almost a life's work. The annual or biennial exhibitions organised during holiday time in the school at St. Jude's from 1881 onwards, were installed in a short time and lasted only for a few days. They relied on paintings lent by artists and the many fashionable people of the Barnetts' acquaintance who could be persuaded to lend. Well publicised though these exhibitions were, they formed only a part of a much more ambitious campaign to ease the life of the local people, a population suffering from poor housing, little ameliorated by employment legislation, provided with an ineffective education system, and above all exposed to a life of drudgery and unemployment with almost no prospect of improvement, in hideous and monotonous streets from which the only relief was the gin palace. Apart from their specifically social work, the Barnetts believed, in accordance with the precepts of the Charity Organisation Society, not in alleviating the symptoms of these social problems but in

Henrietta and Samuel Barnett at the time of their marriage in 1873.

Toynbee Hall before war damage.

The Drawing Room, Toynbee Hall.

Exterior of St. Jude's, Whitechapel showing the mosaic by G. F. Watts.

attacking the causes. Their years in the parish led to the creation of Toynbee Hall, a college-settlement in Whitechapel in which young men from the universities, especially Oxford, would stay for a term of years, organising educational and other activities for the adult population and the young trainee. Henrietta Barnett's life of her husband, *Canon Barnett: His Life, Work and Friends* (1923), illustrates in depth their approach to the problems confronting them, an approach in which the visual arts played a vital role. By contrast to much of the charity doled out from official and private agencies during the nineteenth century, the Barnetts' version, in spite of their refusal to relieve individual cases, seems gentle and humane, Ruskinian in its belief in the need for 'beauty' to become a part of the everyday life of the whole population. The importance of trying to instil a feeling for visual experience in local people stimulated an early form of gallery education, provided not only through the catalogues, with their naive extraction of narrative and moral messages from paintings, but through the voluntary (primarily middle if not upper class) helpers who were pressed into what was felt to be the crucial work of 'explaining' the pictures to their public.

In their own way of life, the Barnetts did not regard it as their duty or as appropriate, to forego the material advantages they could afford. On the contrary, both the rectory at St. Jude's and the Warden's Lodgings in Toynbee Hall were deliberately furnished in as appealing and up-to-date a way as possible (they were fortunate in counting Morris, Crane and C. R. Ashbee among their friends), with the purpose of suggesting the benefits of attractive surroundings to the people from all social backgrounds who were regularly entertained in this setting. In terms of professional promotion, it is clear from Henrietta's book that greatly as he was admired in many circles, her husband's endeavours did not assist him in gaining preferment, and that the canonry which he received in 1893 came much later than (in her view) he deserved. Assiduous as the Barnetts were in cultivating friends in the 'West', one of the prime motives for their activities was the desire to break down social barriers, to achieve the recognition that it was social conditions and privilege, rather than intrinsic ability or virtue, that separated, to use the terms that they themselves employed, 'East' (the East End) from 'West'. It was a theme which in literary terms was explored during this period not only by Walter Besant but by George Bernard Shaw, whose *Pygmalion* reflects a comparable preoccupation. For all their social adeptness and Christian adherence, the Barnetts, like some of those involved with the Ancoats Museum, were more radical than the character of their art exhibitions might suggest.

*   *   *

The South London Art Gallery, though similar in many respects to Ancoats and the Whitechapel, represented in terms of internal conflict, as the essays of Nicola Smith and Leonee Ormond illustrate, a more complex history. It was not driven by the force of a united group of people, as the other institutions were, but by two groups representing distinct interests, and it lacked the single-minded purpose that the other enterprises enjoyed. The South London Art Gallery combined, at least in aspiration and in early days, three types of philanthropic or educational institution: the working men's college or People's Palace, the collection of applied arts for the instruction of craftsmen and apprentices, and the gallery devoted to the fine arts. Although the first two activities were ultimately unable to withstand the impact of the accomplished President of the Royal Academy, they played an important part in the Gallery's early history. The personal differences between Leighton and Rossiter symbolise a deeper conflict: between the individual enterprise of the self-taught man of humble origins aiming to liberate his fellow workers through education on the one hand, and on the other, the single-minded philanthropy of the liberal establishment. The history of the South London Art Gallery epitomises the seductive power of the fine arts in the late nineteenth century as at other periods, capable, as a prime symbol of wealth and power, of excluding from the arena of the public space, or at least marginalising, activities that conveyed less potent codes.

Rossiter's endeavours at the beginning of his career to create libraries and debating clubs in parts of London where no such facilities were provided were part of a broader movement. The relatively unambitious and long-established tradition of the Mechanics' Institute, with its library and exhibitions, had in the 1880s been overshadowed by a much more ambitious undertaking, the People's Palace in the Mile End Road. This extraordinary enterprise, a prime example of the attempt by the ruling classes, alarmed by what was perceived as the threat posed by the district that had come lately to be known as the East End to the existing order, was intended as a centre of pacifying educational and social activity. The Palace, opened by the Queen in 1887, was inspired by the novel of 1882 by Walter Besant, *All Sorts and*

Conditions of Men. Besant imagined the creation by a millionairess of a 'Palace of Delight', in the Mile End Road, where the population of the East End would gain the chance for the first time 'to know what pleasant strolling and resting-place, what delightful interests, what varied recuperation, what sweet diversions there are in life'.[28] The popularity of Besant's novel attracted numerous subscriptions, allowing the realisation of this dream: the Palace, which opened in 1887, was extended the following year. At its height, the building contained a Queen's Hall seating 5,000 people for musical and dramatic events, a library capable of holding 250,000 volumes, a gymnasium and swimming bath and a winter garden, together with a large educational department offering 'a complete series of technical schools with both day and evening classes'.[29] Since 'recreation was the chief purpose of the palace'[30] it organised a busy programme of cultural events, including regular concerts. At the close of 1888 a large exhibition of pictures was arranged of works by past and living British artists, 'the result of an appeal for loans to a number of friends of the institution',[31] a venture clearly inspired by the Whitechapel Art Gallery. In this case a concession to popular taste, very unlike the lofty if popular tone at Whitechapel, was made by the simulations of an Arctic winter, an old-fashioned inn, and a 'huge snowball, entered by a rustic bridge over an artificial lake, at which are stationed Red Riding Hood in costume, and New Year, a little child seated on a white goat, dressed in all white and silver'.[32] The People's Palace, in its recreational aspect, achieved limited success. As fears of revolution subsided, support from the West End for its activities diminished; and from the first the nature of the public for which it was intended was uncertain. Whereas at Whitechapel there was no doubt that the exhibitions were meant for the entire population, especially for the poorest, the People's Palace was directed at the deserving poor, the respectable artisan; and even this audience was not reached on a regular basis, at least in so far as the recreational activities went. From the earliest days the visitors tended to be relatively prosperous and often frivolous, to the

The People's Palace, Mile End Road, London.

The People's Palace, Glasgow, 1900.

Interior of the Winter Garden, People's Palace, Glasgow, c.1900.

concern of the organisers. Within a short time the cultural activities of the Palace became subsidiary to the educational side, the technical schools later forming the basis for Queen Mary's College, a part of London University.

Closer to Camberwell, the Royal Victoria Hall in Waterloo, the origin of the present Old Vic Theatre, was set up by Emma Cons in the 1880s. What she described as 'The People's Palace for South London' organised not only dramatic and musical entertainments in the Temperance Music Hall but such improving opportunities as regular lectures, which attracted around 1,500 people on Saturday nights. Backstage, a 'College for Working Men and Women' was organised, named after the philanthropist Samuel Morley: this offered classes, especially in scientific subjects, a gymnasium and a library.[33] Its aspirations to musical and artistic education were not lost upon Rossiter.

A further People's Palace was opened in Glasgow by the Corporation in 1898, for collections related to the history and industry of the city. It survives, its magnificent winter garden intact.

Rossiter's activities had initially been inspired by the Working Men's College where he had studied as a young man, and this ideal remained strong throughout the earlier phases of the South London Art Gallery. In the premises on the Peckham Road, the first major building was the library and lecture room built by Sir Ernest George, intended as Rossiter put it to revive 'the literary and scientific part of the work, which has for a time been overshadowed by the growth of the art gallery'.[34] The aim was to provide a general cultural education, and to include music which was an important aspect of the Gallery's life. The early lecture series was determined by Rossiter, he being one of the principal speakers. The *Weekly Notes on Art, Nature, Literature and Science*, for November 1891, summarise his aim 'to give in popular language clear and definite accounts of new Works of Art, new Books, new Plays, the progress of Science as human knowledge, and, in Summer, of places where Londoners may have the influence of natural beauty'.[35] The weekly lectures, given at 7.30 p.m. and 'followed by questions and discussion'

'Listening to one of Mr Rossiter's Stories'.

recall the all-encompassing ambitions of the Ancoats Museum: Rossiter's subjects for 1891-92 included 'The Theatre as a Teacher of Morals', 'School Boards and Board Schools', 'A Box of Fossils' and 'Mr. Walter Crane's Picture "Pluto and Persephone"'.[36] With Rossiter's departure, this side of the Gallery's work diminished, indeed practically ended.

The second important aspect of the South London Art Gallery was its role in technical education and in the improvement of popular taste. Just as the Ancoats Museum had included Model Rooms designed by W. A. Benson for Morris and Company, so on a less ambitious level Morris furniture was put on view at Camberwell. Some attempt was made to assemble examples of what was considered the best contemporary design, though the display of cases of Venetian glass ('lent by Venice & Murano'), tiles by William de Morgan framed in wood and hung on the walls, and rolls of wallpaper by Crane, Henry Wilson, and others, supplemented by loans from the South Kensington Museum, hardly constituted an ambitious group of specimens. It was the relationship with the Technical School which developed this aspect of the Galleries most fully.

Following an initiative from the new Borough of Camberwell and the Technical Education Board to set up 'a school of Arts and crafts' in the building about to be erected next to the existing

LECTURES

On Art, Science, and Literature, are given every Sunday evening, from September 1st to May 1st, and occasionally at other times.

The Lectures begin at 7.30 p.m. and are followed by questions and discussion.

Visitors to the Lectures are asked to make some small contribution towards the expenses.

March 3rd

Butterflies & Moths
with Illustrations

March 10th Mr. Balfours
"Foundations of
Belief."

LECTURES TO CHILDREN

Are given every Friday Evening, beginning at 7.15.

The Council will be glad of help from friends willing to take parties of young people to the various London Museums, Art Galleries, &c., on Saturday afternoons, or other convenient times.

Annual Report of South London Art Gallery, 1894.

Catalogue of Works of Art, &c.,

The following Works have been given to the Gallery, and are now the property of the Trustees : Sir F. Leighton, Sir John Lubbock, and W. Rossiter :—

Nos. 1 to 41 are the work of the Donors.

No.	Title.	Donor.
1	Portrait of the Rev. F. D. Maurice	Miss I. Keightley
	(Copy of original by Lowes Dickinson, Esq.)	
2	Portrait of Dean Stanley	... Miss I. Keightley
	(Copy of the original by G. F. Watts, Esq., R.A.)	
3	The Dead Cavalier ...	... S. Holland, Esq.
4	Scotch Moor at Daybreak	... ,, ,,
5	Grandmother's Skein ...	... Miss Newcombe
6	Landscape in Switzerland	... Hon. John Collier
7	Quentin Durward ...	... C. Halle, Esq.
8	Whitby Harbour	... W. Crafton, Esq.
9	The Dead Warrior ...	.. H. Bone, Esq.
10	Westminster Abbey ...	... J. O'Connor, Esq.
11	Boat on the Riviera	,, ,,
12	Early Morning in Thames Valley	
		E. Waterlow, Esq., A.R.A.
13	A Breezy Day	,, ,,
14	Landscape	... A. Quinton, Esq.
15	Meditation	... E. Cooke, Esq.
16	Portrait of George Grote	... Lowes Dickinson, Esq.
17	A Quiet Nook	... Miss K. Amphlett
18	Nine Small Paintings ...	... T. H. Ohrly, Esq.
19	Dinner Time ... ... - ...	... Miss Redgrave
20	The Quarrel	
21	Ten Copies of Old Masters	... Miss L. Twining
22	Chepstow Castle ; Copy of an unfinished drawing	
	by Turner	... Miss Geldart
23	Sunset	... A. Anderson, Esq.
24	Swanage Bay	... C. E. Minifie, Esq.
25	Two Small Studies ...	... C. Collins, Esq.
26	Boy Drinking	... H. S. Tuke, Esq.
27	A Portrait	... ,,
28	Doggie's Breakfast ...	... Mrs. S. Beale
29	Feeding the Cat	... ,,

Catalogue, 1894.

Galleries, the new school was opened in January 1898.[37] Supported by Passmore Edwards, it was intended, in contrast to the teaching given in the traditional academy, to offer practical training. According to the first prospectus, the school was founded 'in order to provide instruction in those branches of design and manipulation which directly bear on the more artistic trades'.[38] Although instruction in drawing was offered, the principal objective in the early days was to encourage crafts people such as builders, decorators, 'Designers in Wall Papers, Textiles and Furniture, and Embroiderers . . . to learn design and those branches of their crafts which, owing to the subdivision of the processes of production, they are unable to learn in the workshop'.[39] In this task, the Galleries were to play an active part: according to the Prospectus, which listed the Galleries' amenities, students were encouraged to copy from the exhibits, and a series of exhibitions (such as the display of engraving techniques organised for the new building in 1898) was arranged 'with a view to the educational requirements of those attending the School'.[40] Many of the leading figures involved in the Gallery participated in the work of the School, including Wyke Bayliss, Linton, Collier and Crane, while C. L. Burns, the first Principal, served also as Curator of the Gallery. This close association between Gallery and School maintained the primarily educational purpose that Rossiter had envisaged, but directed it more specifically towards the applied arts. It was an approach that had little connection with the type of art collection developed under the aegis of Lord Leighton.

*   *   *

For a few years in the 1880s and 1890s, the South London Art Gallery illustrated the powerful working of the system of philanthropic connections in the liberal, and Liberal, establishment of late nineteenth-century Britain. Rossiter, through his boldness in asking for help, and Leighton, through his rich circle of connections, assembled for the South London Art Gallery an influential group of benefactors and artists, whether as donors or lenders of works of art or money. The artists who supported the Gallery belonged in the case of the most famous names to the circle around Leighton – who brought, as Leonee Ormond has illustrated, the support of a number of Royal Academicians – and Burne-Jones. Their friends included both Royal Academicians and numerous artists, well-known and less well-known, associated with the Grosvenor Gallery, which, founded in 1877 in Bond Street, offered a less crowded and more enlightened setting for exhibition than did the Royal Academy. Other than Burne-Jones himself (whose reputation was established at the Grosvenor Gallery), artists associated with the Grosvenor who gave or lent their own works to the South London Gallery included artists in the immediate circle of Burne-Jones: Walter Crane, Val Prinsep, Evelyn de Morgan and T. M. Rooke. Several of the other artists showed regularly at the Grosvenor Gallery.[41] Many of them also showed at the New Gallery, established in 1888 by Hallé and others in reaction against the more commercial character that was being assumed by the Grosvenor Gallery. In addition to these more or less established figures, Camberwell attracted a number of artists of outstanding obscurity, whose willingness to give their pictures can be variously interpreted.

Women played an important role in the activities of the new Gallery, in a way that was still not possible at such conservative institutions as the Royal Academy. The proportion of women giving or lending their work to, for example, the exhibition mounted in 1895 was higher than would have been the case at a contemporary exhibition at the Royal Academy. Of the thirty-eight artists listed as having donated their own work in 1895, nine were women, some established, others scarcely known. Among the lenders the names of women artists also feature, notably Evelyn de Morgan (who later gave her own work), Louise Jopling, a well-established painter specialising in landscape and portraits and the founder of an art school, and Clara Montalba, mostly resident in Venice, one of four artist sisters and a regular exhibitor at the

Evelyn de Morgan, *The Christian Martyr* (No. 41).

well as the education of women, and as a further lender Mrs Winkworth, probably Susanna Winkworth, author and translator, and active in the field of women's education and working class housing.[42] Equally, for women wishing to exercise a talent for organisation, it gave the chance to play an important role in the administration of an institution made additionally respectable by its charitable and non-financial associations. Apart from the vital part played by Mrs Burne-Jones and Mrs Watts, women contributed significantly to the development of the Gallery, and their contribution was recognised in the composition of the Council: in 1890 a quarter of its twenty members were female.

Rossiter and Leighton's support was strengthened by a network of well-connected philanthropists and Liberal politicians. Apart from Baroness Burdett Coutts, these names included (as a trustee) Sir John Lubbock, later created Lord Avebury, Liberal Member of Parliament for the University of London from 1880 to 1900, prominent banker and President of the Society of Antiquaries and the Royal Society; 'Miss Hill' – presumably the redoubtable Octavia Hill, Secretary of the Working Men's College from 1856, pioneer of housing reform (a cause in which she succeeded in interesting Ruskin) and a joint founder of the National Trust, whose analogous activities included the promotion in the 'Red Cross Hall' in Southwark of depictions of the heroic deeds of ordinary people; Lord Monkswell, son of a prominent Liberal politician and himself Lord-in-Waiting to the Queen and Under-Secretary of State for War in 1895, an amateur painter with a further painter, John Collier as a son (both gave works to the Gallery); Sir Donald Currie, Liberal MP, philanthropist and picture collector; and Cyril Flower, Lord Battersea. Battersea was another Liberal politician (and a minister under Gladstone's last administration), President of the Recreative Evening School Association, and a collector of Renaissance and Pre-Raphaelite paintings; his wife, a Rothschild, was an active supporter of the Barnetts. The fund-raising activities of the Gallery, as it became established,

Grosvenor and New Galleries. The Gallery attracted the support of a number of women interested in women's rights: notably as a lender Anna Swanwick, author and translator, whose interest in social questions included raising the moral and intellectual tone of the working class as

Lord Battersea (pastel by Frederick Sandys, Norwich Castle).

ment in its affairs of Lubbock and Burdett Coutts that persuaded Passmore Edwards to make the donation which allowed the building to be completed.

The supporters of the Gallery were not limited to the merely rich and powerful: the most advanced artistic circles of the time were involved in its foundation and support. The interest in the Gallery shown by Crane and Burne-Jones involved prominent patrons of the Arts and Crafts Movement and the Aesthetic Movement in its affairs, notably the Earl of Carlisle, the nobleman-artist for whom Philip Webb built a house at 1 Palace Green, Kensington, and who gave commissions to Burne-Jones, Crane and Morris, and the Hon. Percy Wyndham, a further patron of Webb and his friends.[44] Other supporters included the venerable J. C. Robinson, former Curator of the South Kensington Museum and a leading figure in the creation of its early collections; and the collector E. A. Ionides, who left his pictures to South Kensington and was also a patron of the Webb-Morris circle. In addition to members of the South Kensington-Little Holland House set, other celebrities were involved, including J. W. Cross, who made a donation in memory of his wife George Eliot; the dealer Michael Colnaghi, expert on Dutch and Flemish painting, champion of the Barbizon school and patron of the National Gallery, who lent a dozen British and foreign paintings; and Mr and Mrs Rudyard Kipling, he lending eleven paintings, while she gave a collection of curiosities.[45] Like the Whitechapel, the Camberwell institution was active in invoking the support of well-known and glamorous figures: leading representatives of the stage – a newly respectable profession – who gave help included, in addition to Irving, Herbert Beerbohm Tree. For a brief period (much briefer than that enjoyed at the Whitechapel Art Gallery as a result of the activities of the indefatigable Barnetts), the Gallery attracted support among the most cultivated, as well as the wealthiest, circles in the country.

*　*　*

Unlike the Ancoats Museum or the White-

represented an equally remarkable progression from the early days of the shops and warehouses used as temporary premises: the *Report of a Public Meeting*, a pamphlet produced in 1890 to record a meeting held on behalf of the Gallery at the Royal Society of British Artists at which Sir Henry Irving, leading tragic actor of the day, was the principal speaker, listed among the contributors three Rothschilds, (including Lord Rothschild, who as Sir Nathaniel was the first Jewish (Liberal) Member of Parliament and had become a leading member of society), and the Duke of Westminster (an enthusiastic collector, who regularly opened Grosvenor House, with its outstanding gallery, to parties of craftsmen on educational visits).[43] The reputation lent by these prominent supporters encouraged others to give too: it was the involve-

chapel Art Gallery, the South London Art Gallery retains its original collection in its original building – or, at least, part of its collection in part of its building. It is not easy to assess the Gallery's original holdings: many of the works listed in the 1895 catalogue and in the Gallery's accession book have disappeared, and the 1895 catalogue is a confused and inaccurate compilation. Nevertheless, enough survives, with sufficient documentation, to convey the character of this collection: idiosyncratic, occasionally distinguished, sometimes reach-me-down.

The South London Art Gallery had no purchase fund, and its acquisition policy was, of necessity, reactive, depending on donations by artists and patrons. With the exception of a few temporary loans, it contained no foreign paintings other than a handful of copies of Old Masters, and no attempt was made to display British paintings of the past, other than a dim copy of a Turner drawing. The Hogarth of *The Assembly at Wanstead House* (sold to the Tate Gallery in 1983) which was bequeathed in 1899, was the only work of any substance that was not, broadly speaking, contemporary. The early catalogues indicate, however, that the idea of a 'museum' consisting entirely of reproductions was explored in the early days, even though the lack of continued organisation prevented this idea from being realised in any very concrete way. Miss Twining's copies of ten 'Old Masters', and the photographs of Wedgwood pottery, 'Carvings at South Kensington Museum' and 'Statuary by Thorwaldsen'[46] represented a lacklustre attempt to create a type of collection which, although a full-blown example of the museum of historical reproductions was created at the Harris Museum at Preston as late as 1893, by the 1890s was becoming old-fashioned.

Some artists gave generously, like T. M. Rooke; some gave or lent almost too generously, like Clara Montalba, recorded in 1895 as having lent 28 works including landscapes not only from her own easel but from those of her siblings Ellen, Hilda and Anthony; while one or two of the most distinguished participants in the enterprise (notably Leighton) parted only with prints and very minor

oils, though Watts was more generous. Edward Burne-Jones appears to have given none of his own work although Rossiter received, in memory of his wife, *Ministering Angels* from the artist. His son, Philip Burne-Jones, also gave numerous pictures. In spite of this necessarily arbitrary approach, the collection assumed a distinct character. This was determined partly by the Little Holland House associations of some of the principal participants, which stimulated the donation of allegorical and Biblical works by Evelyn de Morgan, Rooke and Watts. The sophisticated character of these offerings was more than counterbalanced by the improving nature of many of the works, close in character to the paintings and drawings to be seen at the Ancoats Museum, and close also to the type of collection on view in the emerging municipal art galleries of nineteenth-century Britain. Following Ruskin's recommendation that the museum intended 'for *simple* persons' should offer 'the manifestation to them of what is lovely in the life of Nature, and heroic in the life of Men',[47] there was some representation of British history, capable according to the mores of the time of arousing a feeling for the finest national values in the beholder. Whereas Hallé's *Quentin Durward* referred to the genre of the Scott novel, such ambitious works as Ford Madox Brown's *The Body of Harold* or Val Prinsep's *Death of Siward* – the deaths of warriors feature largely in this collection – reflected the tradition of the portrayal of native virtue. Prinsep's work recalled the paintings in the Central Hall at Wallington, in Northumberland, where the depictions of the Northumbrian past and the botanical decoration had been inspired by Ruskin. Ruskin's insistence that 'the proper occupation of his life' had been to 'record . . . great existing art, English and foreign . . . liable more and more every hour to find destruction by the restorer, or by the various rages and interests of a manufacturing population'[48] was reflected in the Gallery, as at Ancoats, by depictions of historic buildings. They included the unattributed *Room where Shakespeare was born*[49] as well as etchings, and an oil, of Westminster Abbey, the epitome of English monarchical culture and history. The

T. M. Rooke, *Jephthah's Daughter* (No. 50).

Below: C. E. Hallé, *Quentin Durward* (No. 29). Below: G. F. Watts, *The Open Door* (No. 63).

Val Prinsep, *The Death of Siward* (No. 47).

Below: H. J. Boddington, *Sketch from Nature* (No. 5).

depiction of fine unspoilt landscape was regarded by Ruskin and his followers as of prime importance, allowing those who could not travel at least to glimpse the beauty of foreign scenery: it was an ideal that the Barnetts had actually realised, by leading their parishioners in groups on strenuous foreign holidays. The South London Art Gallery showed numerous foreign scenes, more or less exotic: Collier's *Switzerland*, Leighton's *Algiers*, Wyke Bayliss's *Rheims*, Ellis's *Bruges* and *Egypt*, and assorted others.

At Ancoats, Whitechapel and Camberwell, the association between the art museum and a practical pastoralism in the form of escape from the city to the countryside, for the day in the case of adults or longer for children, was close. Like Henrietta Barnett, Mrs Rossiter was active in this field: in the centre of the Gallery stood, in 1895, a marble memorial celebrating her achievements. Inscribed 'Elizabeth Rossiter, Founder of Country Life for Poor Town Children, 1836-1888', it listed the places where between 1871 and 1887 she organised regular holidays for children who in most cases had never glimpsed hedge or cow. The incidence of rural scenes, generally English, generally sunny and always appealing, was therefore high in the permanent collection and even more so among the loans. A collection of this sort followed Ruskin's stipulation that a museum must manifest to its simple visitors the 'beauty and life of all things, and creatures in their perfectness'.[50] In such a museum there was no place for gloom, other than over the death of mediaeval warriors. Depictions of working class life were rare even at a time when such frank portrayals of deprivation as Fildes' *Applicants for Admission to a Casual Ward*, of 1874, were extremely popular; everyday scenes were generally presented through such works as Mrs S. Beale's *Doggie's Breakfast*.

An individual character was given to the collection by the inclusion of a number of portraits of radical heroes, or proponents of popular education, balancing the loyal (but not, from the nature of its subject-matter, presumably assertively royalist) *The Queen and Lord Beaconsfield*. In addition to (understandably) anonymous portraits of John

Whitechapel Art Gallery, c.1901.

Wilkes and William Cobbett, champions of the rights of the ordinary citizen, the portraits included depictions of F. D. Maurice, the founder of the Working Men's College from which the inspiration of the Gallery derived, and a miscellaneous group of intellectuals associated with education.[51] One may suppose that the inclusion of at least some of these figures (following a precedent set at Ancoats, which contained portraits of Richard Cobden and John Bright, both radical politicians with strong connections in the northeast) reflected what were considered in some circles to be Rossiter's pronounced left-wing sympathies, and that they constituted in miniature a radical, or at least liberal, pantheon.

* * *

In terms of its building and installation, the South London Art Gallery represented a much more ambitious enterprise than the Ancoats Museum or the Whitechapel exhibitions in their early days. In its final form it can be compared in scale and ambition to the Whitechapel Art Gallery and the Horniman Museum, Forest Hill, London, both of which opened in 1901 in structures designed by C. Harrison Townsend. In the case of these two institutions and of the South London Art Gallery the building contained an ambitious façade fronting utilitarian brick blocks: all three interiors consisted of two major halls with various subsidiary rooms. The South London Art Gallery's façade is less idiosyncratic than those of Harrison Townsend, but the accommodation provided was more extensive than is perceived by the present-day visitor, who sees only a corridor and one large gallery. A plan of 1894, before the Maurice Adams elevation to the Peckham Road was added, illustrates the extent of the Gallery.[52] It contained the surviving 'Art Gallery', with its fine top lighting, a 'Small Museum' room, and the 'Lecture Hall, Library and Reading Room', recently added by Sir Ernest George – a reminder of the early character of the institution, intended not just as a place for showing pictures but as an educational institute for the working population. George, a successful London and country house architect, with a personal interest in the Gallery (he contributed to its funds), designed an imposing room, 80 by 34 feet, in a baronial style, with a queen post roof and a minstrels' gallery at the north end, containing a podium for the lecturer. This ambitious construction (paid for by Passmore Edwards) was decorated with improving slogans. In addition to this room (destroyed in World War II), the building contained a side-lit 'black and white room' for the display of engravings, and a room for 'decorative objects'. By 1898, the garden, on which it was hoped that an extension might one day be erected, was arranged in four sections of lawn around a fountain, and was intended to be used for drawing by students from the art school. At its height, this was an ambitious and handsome ensemble, reflecting the hope of Rossiter that the Gallery might become 'the National Gallery of South London – an actual part of the National Gallery, or of South Kensington Museum, as is Bethnal Green Museum', and publicly funded.[53]

The arrangement of the exhibits in the 1890s showed a comparable sophistication, as the leaflet published by the Borough of Camberwell soon after it took control of the Gallery illustrates. This was no higgledy-piggledy display like the early Whitechapel or Ancoats, since the dominant figures at the South London Art Gallery included artists schooled in the refined standards of the Grosvenor Gallery. The 'Ruskin Room' must have

been an impressive interior, with its (surviving) top lighting, elegant gas fittings (essential for a space, that was, like the South Kensington Museum but not the National Gallery, open regularly in the evening) and the inlaid parquet floor by Walter Crane, its central decorative panel adorned with the legend 'The Source of Art is in the Life of a People'. As was frequently the case at this period in large art galleries, when the use of rooms of overpowering size and the arrangement of paintings primarily for architectural effect had become unfashionable, the walls of both the main rooms were divided into two broad bands, the paintings being restricted to the lower band. The decoration was carried out to a scheme suggested by Burne-Jones and Wyke Bayliss:[54] this may have been the one mentioned in 1895, when the walls were covered in 'Paper-hangings' donated by Messrs. W. Woollams & Co. in the main room, and by the well-established firm of wallpaper designers, Jeffreys & Co., in the side gallery. What would today be called sponsorship extended to the iron doors – considered vital for fire-proofing – and the installation of the Crane floor.[55] As for the pictures in the 'Ruskin Gallery', they were arranged in symmetrical rows on the north wall facing the arriving visitor, and with a degree of freedom on the side walls, where the pattern was determined by the position of the various picture rails. Since fully hung walls were considered old-fashioned and prejudicial to appreciation of paintings, the organisers followed up-to-date principles: 'Only two lines of pictures are hung in the Gallery, which, with a space between, ensures each picture being seen to the greatest advantage'.[56] The Engraving Gallery was arranged loosely, with the prints placed in large white mounts in unmoulded plain or stained wooden frames in the manner by then popularised through Whistler, in contrast to the earlier gold frames. The Lecture Room or 'Passmore Edwards Gallery' aspired to less elegance, though it too contained numerous paintings, some of considerable size. Its parquet floor was covered in show cases and desk cases, displaying objects from the museum collection.

In 1895 the galleries were still fronted on the

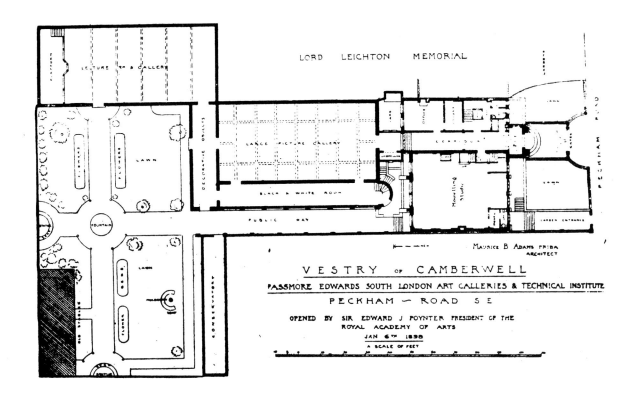

LORD LEICHTON MEMORIAL

VESTRY OF CAMBERWELL

PASSMORE EDWARDS SOUTH LONDON ART GALLERIES & TECHNICAL INSTITUTE

PECKHAM — ROAD S E

OPENED BY SIR EDWARD J POYNTER PRESIDENT OF THE
ROYAL ACADEMY OF ARTS

JAN 6TH 1898

A SCALE OF FEET

MAURICE B ADAMS FRIBA
ARCHITECT

The Ruskin Gallery ('Large Picture Gallery'), c.1900.

The Passmore Edwards Gallery,
Building News, 6th October 1893.

Peckham Road by an entrance lobby and vestibule squeezed into a narrow space beside the brick building known as Portland House and occupied by Rossiter. The extension between 1896 and 1898 into the Technical School radically affected the Gallery's character. The new building was, again, paid for by Passmore Edwards, whose help with new building projects led to the construction of numerous libraries and museums in deprived areas of large cities: his interest in this area of south London was apparent from his support for numerous new libraries.[57] Reports of the proceedings at the laying of the foundation stone, in March 1893, give some impression of his ideals. In response to G. F. Watts' opening speech, which stressed that the South London Art Gallery complemented the 'notable work' being done by Passmore Edwards in 'supplying additional facilities for literary and art enlightenment', the philanthropist emphasised his interest in the social aspects of the new establishment, which he analysed in terms of its contribution to the moral well being of the inhabitants of south London, rather than the quality of its collections. It was, he felt, 'desirable that additional opportunities for art education and recreation from art resources should be provided, and particularly in dreary and monotonous South London', and he was persuaded to assist by the fact that the institution was to be open on Sundays, that it would welcome children, and that it would establish an association with a Technical School. Since 'such means of art culture and art recreation, and especially on the south side of the Thames, had been few and far between', the Gallery 'assisted to supply a marked deficiency'.[58] Although Passmore Edwards favoured libraries, he did support the construction of other museums and galleries. In the East End he had already paid for the erection in 1891-2 of the Whitechapel Public Library and Museum; in 1898 he was to make a major contribution towards the cost of the West Ham Museum (now the Passmore Edwards Museum) which as the 'permanent home of the Essex Field Club' would gather and distribute information on the 'biology, geology, typography, meteorology, eth-

nology and archaeology of Essex . . .'[59] As at Camberwell, this institution was intended to be intimately linked with the newly built library and technical institute.

The involvement of Passmore Edwards in the 1896 scheme brought with it the choice of architect. Maurice B. Adams (1849-1933), who designed the new buildings for the Technical Institute and the front section of the Galleries to include an entrance vestibule, an office for the curator and a cloak room all behind one facade, was closely associated with this patron. For over fifty years Adams served on the staff of *Building News*, which Passmore Edwards owned, and their sympathy for one another is apparent from the fact that Adams designed several libraries funded by Passmore Edwards.[60] Adams was an enthusiastic proponent of the style known as Queen Anne, a spirited reordering of seventeenth- and eighteenth-century English (and sometimes Flemish) architectural motifs, with an emphasis on red brick and white-painted woodwork, and championed the style in *Building News*. Bedford Park, the planned suburb in west London which was one of the key achievements of the Queen Anne manner as of late nineteenth-century garden city planning, provided Adams with a home and with numerous commissions: he completed the church there and designed many of the houses. Adams was a well-regarded figure internationally, gaining commissions in the United States and in Australia; and his interest in historic buildings was apparent from his involvement, as secretary for many years, with the Royal Architectural Museum, in Westminster, and with such work as the restoration of the great Jacobean house, Blickling Hall, in Norfolk. Such a man was well prepared for this particular commission: Bedford Park included among its inhabitants such artist-supporters of the South London Art Gallery as T. M. Rooke and F. Hamilton Jackson, Principal of the nearby Chiswick School of Art, and was known for its progressive and aesthetic sympathies, in accordance with the programme of the new Gallery.

Adams designed an impressive yet welcoming elevation, a suitable enhancement of a part of

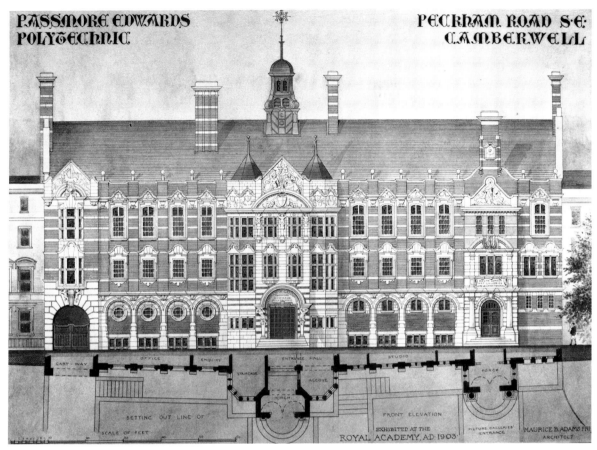

M. B. Adams, *Elevation of Gallery.*

London which in Rossiter's view was notably deficient in this regard: he called South London 'a great intellectual desert, with miles upon miles of flat, square, ugly houses, with scarce any beauty of architecture, and with absolutely no public buildings'.[61] The creation of a building of this quality on the Peckham Road, one of the main thoroughfares of Camberwell, suggested an attempt to introduce some civic dignity and a centre in a featureless district. Adams' plans changed from the first scheme of 1896, published in the *Building News*,[62] to the building as executed. The most significant change was the relocation of the principal entrance. In the 1896 proposal this was placed on the axis of the 'First Gallery', with a corridor leading from main door to gallery entrance, and with

a modelling studio reached via this corridor and to the arriving visitor's left. Though the sculpture at roof level, dedicated to Architecture, Painting and Sculpture, could apply to both the principal uses of the building, the inscription in the cartouche over the door in the 1896 scheme made it clear that the façade was dedicated firstly to the Gallery and only secondly to the Technical Institute. As built, the emphasis was altered radically. Adams' building for the Gallery has become subsidiary to a much larger edifice for the Technical College, with an independent entrance via a boldly protruding arch supported by atlantes, and an assertively decorative study of the use of curved windows in an adapted Tudor manner. The entrance to the Gallery had become relatively

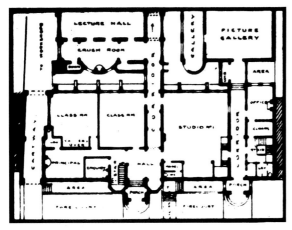

M. B. Adams, *Plan of Gallery.*

inconspicuous, anticipating the process by which the Gallery was to be pushed, if not out of its nest, at least to the side, by its cuckoo of an art school. As the author of books on *Old English Houses and Mansions* and *Artists' Homes*, Adams designed what was described as a 'Renaissance' building, a playful version of the solemnly exuberant Wren Revival architecture popular at the time. The care given to the building extended to the surrounding ironwork, especially to the ornamental railings and gates, and to W. Goscombe John's sculptural decoration.

* * *

In a sense, all three of these innovative showplaces failed, at least in sustaining their original objectives. With the construction of its new building, the Whitechapel Art Gallery shifted from its original purpose of providing art for dwellers in the slums to the organisation of contemporary exhibitions, even though links with its local community have remained strong. The Manchester Art Museum continued in existence in Ancoats Hall until 1954, gradually dwindling. In 1945 the tireless curator, Bertha Hindshaw, who for many years strove to maintain the museum's role as a teaching facility for children, was forced to write 'We are in a ghastly state here . . . The rain is com-

ing in in so many places and the staircase is terrible. We have all our buckets in use catching rainfall . . . Meanwhile we do what we can!'[63] The Queen's Park Museum, the first home of the Manchester Art Museum, a purpose-built gallery of 1874, sited originally in the highly cultivated ornamental gardens which were one of the earliest public parks in Britain and were intended with the museum to offer pleasure to the residents of a poor neighbourhood, has been closed for twenty years, its park reduced to a wasteland. As for the South London Art Gallery, the confusion of purpose associated with its early days has over the years borne ambiguous fruit. For many years after the Second World War it served neither as a centre of activity for the local population nor as a service for the adjacent Art School; it housed, and still does, three incongruous collections – the Victorian works of art, a twentieth century British collection associated with artists working at Camberwell, and the Southwark topographical collection – which by the nature of the building cannot be shown on anything more than a very occasional basis. Though its future is now brighter, it is unlikely, in any but the most general way, to be able to fulfil its founders' ambitions.

* * *

But the work of these pioneers – for pioneers Horsfall and the Barnetts and Rossiter were, however one may disapprove of their application of the fine arts – was not altogether in vain. Their activities opened the question of the relationship between the visual arts and the general public in a way that the many other museums of the time in Britain seldom attempted: in particular they explored the issue of the visual arts in relation to children. Theirs were all places to which children were welcome, into which the young were sometimes literally dragged; and it was Horsfall's museum and his energetic lobbying on its behalf which in 1895 persuaded the Board of Education to allow school visits to museums to be counted as part of a school's formal activities. Equally it was Horsfall who through his organisation of a school loan scheme instituted a system which, old-fashioned as it may now seem, in its day contributed to the life of many schools. In a society in which the fine arts were still generally, though not exclusively, regarded as part of the cultural capital of the rich and educated, these eccentric individualists began, however falteringly and ineptly, to question that expectation. Those of us who, however faltering and inept we may be ourselves, participate in the educational life of the modern museum, have reason to salute them.

FOOTNOTES

1. See H. Meller, *Leisure and the Changing City*, 1976.
2. Walter Besant, *All Sorts and Conditions of Men*, 1882, p.18.
3. F. Borzello, *Civilising Caliban: The Misuse of Art 1875-1980*, 1987.
4. M. Harrison, 'Art and Philanthropy: T. C. Horsfall and the Manchester Art Museum', in *City, Class and Culture*, eds. A. Kidd and K. Roberts, 1985, and M. Harrison, 'Ancoats Art Museum' in *Manchester Region History Review*, 1993, VII, pp.63-72.
5. Parliamentary Select Committee, *Report*, 1841, p.iv.
6. Department of Science and Art, *Annual Report*, 1858, p.79.
7. ibid, p.80.
8. D. S. A., 1865, pp.7-8.
9. D. S. A., 1866, p.5.
10. Anthony Burton, lecture, *Department of Science and Art and the Bethnal Green Museum* (1982).
11. ibid, p.12.
12. 'Life without industry is guilt and industry without art is brutality'.
13. J. Ruskin XIX, *Modern Art*, 1867, p.219.
14. J. Ruskin XIII, *Picture Galleries - Their Functions and Formation*, 1857, p.547.
15. Ruskin, 1867, p.226.
16. J. Ruskin XXXIV, *A Museum or Picture Gallery: Its Function and Its Formation*, 1880, p.250.
17. Ruskin, 1857, p.548.
18. Ruskin, 1867, p.219.
19. Ruskin, 1880, p.247.
20. ibid, pp.251-252.
21. They were related to Evelyn de Morgan, one of the artists involved with the South London Art Gallery.
22. *A Description of the Work of the Manchester Art Museum, Ancoats Hall*, 1895, p.1.
23. The ms catalogue of the collection, made in 1918, survives in the archives of the Manchester City Art Gallery.
24. See T. C. Horsfall, *Handbook to the Manchester Art Museum*, 1886, and Harrison, 1985.
25. T. C. Horsfall, *An Art Gallery for Manchester*, 1877, p.5.
26. ibid, p.4.
27. His Museum correspondence is in the Manchester City Art Gallery's archives.
28. Besant, 1882, p.133.
29. E. Bisland, 'The People's Palace in London' in *The Cosmopolitan*, January 1891, p.265.
30. ibid, p.262.
31. *East London Advertiser* quoted in W. Fishman, *East End 1888*, 1989, p.315.
32. ibid.
33. See G. Rowell, *The Old Vic Theatre: a History*, 1993, esp. pp.72ff.
34. Rossiter, 1893, p.6.
35. W. Rossiter, *Weekly Notes*, November 1891.
36. Rossiter, 1891.
37. Minutes of the London County Council Advisory Sub-Committee of Camberwell School of Arts and Crafts, Camberwell College of Arts archives.
38. Camberwell School Prospectus, 1898, Introduction, p.3.
39. ibid.
40. ibid.
41. They included Herbert Bone, C. L. Burns, Samuel Carter (whose work was admired by Ruskin), Tristram Ellis, C. E. Hallé (whose father the musician Charles Hallé gave regular free concerts at the Ancoats Museum), F. H. Jackson, A. W. Parsons, Everton Sainsbury, H. S. Tuke, E. A. Waterlow, and W. M. Wyllie - in all, a substantial proportion of the total.
42. Susanna Winkworth died in 1884, but the loan, recorded in 1895, might well have remained on deposit at the Gallery for over a decade.
43. S. L. A. G., 1890, p.8.
44. S. L. A. G., 1891.
45. ibid.
46. S. L. A. G., 1895, nos. 94-96.
47. Ruskin, 1880, p.251.
48. Ruskin, 1881, p.36.
49. S. L. A. G., 1895, no.86; present whereabouts unknown.
50. Ruskin, 1880, p.252.
51. George Grote, historian of Greece and ardent proponent of political freedom; Arthur Stanley, Dean of Westminster, writer and leader of the most liberal wing of the Church of England; Sir Richard Owen, widely-known zoologist and curator of the natural history collections of the British Museum; and the physicist G. G. Stokes.
52. *Plan of Buildings and Guide of South London Art Gallery*, 1894.
53. Rossiter, 1893, p.5.
54. *Building News*, 7 January 1898.
55. S. L. A. G., 1895, p.16.
56. S. L. A. G., *Introduction*, n. d.
57. In Borough Road, Southwark (1898), at Lordship Lane, East Dulwich (1896) and at Wells Way, Camberwell (1902), among others.
58. J. Macdonald, *Passmore Edwards Institutions*, 1900, p.6.
59. ibid, pp.60-61.
60. At Acton, Shepherds Bush and St. George's-in-the-East, as well as in Camberwell.
61. Rossiter, 1893, p.6.
62. B. N., 10 April 1896.
63. Bertha Hindshaw to the Director, 8 February 1945, letter in Manchester City Art Gallery archives.

George Lance, *Grandmother's Blessing* (S.L.G.).

64

Caroline Arscott

Sentimentality in Victorian Paintings

In this essay I will suggest that a key boundary in aesthetics is that between sentiment and the sentimental, and that this borderline was one that was crucial for the political ramifications of late nineteenth century aesthetics. In the latter half of the Victorian period aesthetics served, not the interests of a newly enfranchised bourgeoisie, but the interests of an established middle class preoccupied with containing and pacifying its own working class. It is possible to discriminate, broadly, between models of analysis, which we can trace back to Kant, in which the mind and body are rigidly separated, and those we can align with Rousseau, in which a moral response is said to inhere in a physical response of empathy. Terry Eagleton, in *The Ideology of the Aesthetic*, points to a conservative tradition in British aesthetic commentary which stresses the continuities between the physical and the moral rather than insisting on an absolute rupture between them. Shaftesbury, Hume, Burke and Arnold, each in a different way, make a case for the dependence of reason and judgement on physical response. Spontaneous individual response can thus be expected to buttress or perpetuate the political order.[1]

The debates of the 1870s to 1890s in England saw the re-emergence of a notion of the autonomy of art. The most dramatic moment of confrontation was that between Whistler and Ruskin in the trial of 1878, where Whistler sued Ruskin for his disparaging remarks concerning a work shown at the Grosvenor Gallery.[2] The confrontation was between Ruskin's notion of moral value linked to extrinsic truth and Whistler's notion of aesthetic value, intrinsic in the work and independent of moral values. Whistler, in a further elaboration of his position in his *Ten O'Clock Lecture* of 1885, argued that art cannot be charged with a social

mission, nor can it be expected to tell a story, because beauty is a matter of formal harmony and art is, properly, entirely self-referential.[3] The senses are involved, but in isolation from their everyday uses. It became a matter of importance to the Aesthetic Movement to stress a hierarchy among the senses. Sight and hearing were held to be the most elevated and most abstract, and so painting and music could be perceived sensorially without being vitiated by the sensual. As Kestner has pointed out, the artists Poynter and Leighton, in their addresses to Royal Academy students, echo or foretell some of these tenets.[4] Poynter took issue with Ruskin's insistence that moral considerations are the foundation of our appreciation of the beautiful. He admits that it may be true that we, as viewers, can be prompted to moral reflection in response to the beauties of nature, but the beauty of an art work is intrinsic and has nothing to do with these extrinsic considerations:

'If then I have made my meaning clear, I shall be understood to have said that the idea must be expressed in the work of art, and not merely exist in the mind of the artist, or be supplied by that of the beholder; that the moral nature of beauty is of a kind that cannot be expressed in painting or sculpture; that therefore, as far as art is concerned, ideas of beauty are and must be purely aesthetic.'[5]

Leighton too argues against the notion that art is, in its essence, harnessed to morality. He implicitly opposes Ruskin's arguments about the moral and aesthetic degeneration of the renaissance. He states that art is not best fitted to convey ethical truths. This he says is the province of Speech. His addresses were delivered from 1879 to 1893 and were published in 1896. By the 1880s and 1890s we can see that the arguments for the purity of aesthetics had gained considerable ground. The vocabulary of art criticism had generally become far more technical, as critics concerned themselves primarily with questions of harmony of form. We can make a connection between the emergence of art history as a separate specialist discipline in the latter part of the century, the use of specialised art language and this effort to sunder aesthetics from morality.

The modernist positions that were developed by Fry and Bell in the twentieth century, with their vehement opposition to any literary component in the visual arts, can be seen to rest on the separation of art from society proclaimed by the Aesthetic Movement. A modernist perspective can however lead us to see this victory of Whistler over Ruskin as more complete than it was in fact. A project such as the South London Art Gallery invites us to look again at the 1880s and 1890s and to reconsider the balance between a social aesthetic and an entirely hermetic aesthetic in art theory and criticism of the period. Clearly the artists and patrons involved with the Gallery considered that art had a role to play in teaching and improving the working population. Was it just in the case of working class viewers that there was still felt to be a role for didactic art and that Ruskin was wheeled in? Did the advanced thinkers of the day indulge in retrocriticism for the occasion, resort to some aesthetic slumming and condone story-telling and sentimentality south of the river? I think there is an element of this in the presentation of this collection and in other parallel ventures such as the Whitechapel Fine Art Exhibitions. There was an attempt to include works that were adapted to the (presumed) limited powers of the audience. Genre subjects: rural life and labour, children and animal paintings were considered especially suitable. In the case of the Whitechapel, as Frances Borzello has shown, catalogue explanations were used to moralise the works, whatever the type of picture. A story was told: the viewer was encouraged to see the scene as the acting out of virtue in some form. She cites the catalogue entry for a picture in the 1887 Whitechapel Fine Art Exhibition:

'Notice, beside the skilful painting – how the artist has put womanhood into the cow, and childhood into the calf.'[6] Maternal feeling and family affections could be read off from animal painting and would encourage similar affections in the viewers. Thus the picture gallery would offer a series of emotional experiences that could be converted into lessons in conduct.

In the South London Art Gallery collection a number of works lend themselves to this kind of reading. The painting by T. S. Cooper of a ewe with her two identical lambs, *Twins* of 1861, perhaps speaks of endurance and the affections of a family group in adversity. They lie close to the bank in the cold wind, protected by their shaggy coats. The lambs are identical in shape and in the way they curl round to their mother, but they are differentiated in colour. These creatures, adapted for the rigours of the weather and open country, seem to partake of the substance of the landscape itself. Their rough wool is textured like the scrubby grass, but is soft and balloons out like the clouds above them. The cloud forms split off into ancillary masses. The margin of the grass meanders, almost producing divisions, and yet all the areas are linked. This theme of spreading and splitting is picked up in the meandering river on the left that is on the way to creating an ox-bow lake. In the bodies of the sheep it is most insistently worked out. The two lambs are so close that they could be thought to be twin segments of one form, and the tail of the lamb on the left links their forms to that of the mother. Within the body of the ewe the parting of the wool along the back indicates the possibility of division, as does the tail that lies at her back like a small replica of her shaggy body. In the lambs this parting and the fluffy tail are repeated twice over. The theme is not just one of reproduction but one of division and sub-division. The closeness of the family group, and the inference of maternal care and infantile devotion, depends upon the suggestion that these organic forms cohere as they multiply, and that any replication preserves the unity of substance. The sentiment of the painting, and its moral potential, rests on a response to the formula of

T. S. Cooper, *Twins* (S.L.G.).

mother plus offspring which is ultimately anthropomorphic. We may try to read their facial expressions to give us an emotional entry. Certainly we read the bodily stance of these low-lying creatures and understand their patience and endurance. But additionally there is a special pleasure in seeing twins and a particular attraction in such soft and woolly lambs and these pleasures accent the anthropomorphic reading.

In Alice Havers's *Trouble* of 1882 we see a human family in adversity. In a dingy upstairs apartment a mother and four children are gathered. The mother has a dead or dying son on her lap. She sends out an older lad for help. A neighbour approaches up the stairs bearing a jug and a cloth. One younger ragged child shrinks into a shadowy corner in distress but the older children are rallying round. The elder daughter, hollow-eyed like her mother, peels off the sick boy's sock and gazes at him with an intense expression of sorrow and love, mingled with awe. The undressing of the boy seems to move him from the quotidian environment. The muffling fabrics and textures of the setting, from the wretched scrap of carpet to the coarse laundry strung across the window, are stripped away to reveal pallid flesh. We are confronted with bare human necessity and the stubborn matter that is the fleshly envelope of the soul. The pose of the mother and son recalls a *Pietà* but the anxious mother issuing instructions has none of the tender reverence of a Mary grieving for the dead Christ. Instead that role is taken on by the

Alice Havers, *Trouble* (S.L.G.).

Below: Samuel Carter, *Rabbits* (No. 19).

daughter. The sponging of a fevered body or the washing of a corpse takes on connotations of the cleansing of the world from sin. The basin and jug can refer to baptism as well as to the humdrum tasks of the sickroom and the drudgery of taking in laundry. Homely themes of motherly love, filial duty, neighbourliness, hard work, and managing against the odds, meet grander themes of life and death, the human and the divine, sin and salvation. The domestic familiarity of the scene and the naturalism, here a harsh and demonstrative realism rather than an illusionistic naturalism, might be expected to make the simpler themes immediately and universally available. The intense emotions called up by the situation could be a route in to the more profound messages.

Human and animal groups are also used to depict much more settled family scenes. Samuel Carter's *Rabbits* and George Lance's *Grandmother's Blessing* give us mothers with their offspring. In these cases texture is linked, not with the harsh realities of mortal existence, but with the delight and comfort of the maternal body. The gloss and sheen of the strokable fur of these splendid rabbits is recreated vividly and is set off by the contrasting liquid depths of the large dark eyes and the fragile shiny wisps of dry grasses that surround them. The lustrous fur promises us warmth and a cushiony softness. It is most vivid on the top of the head of the centrally placed bunny and on the mother rabbit's dewlap: that comfortable ring of fat on which her head settles. The fur painting evokes a substance that is fascinating both for its smooth and even surface, accentuated when it is stroked flat along the body, and for its fluffy depths, revealed when the surface is bent or the stroking goes against the grain. In these lop-ears the ears that lie back against the body mimic the smooth-lying fur and the springing ears of the young that have not developed lop-ears mimic the capability of fur to bounce back or be ruffled. One mottled rabbit in the foreground is a half-lop with ears pointing two ways: one drooping and one raised ear. The achievement of naturalism is to offer pleasures of the surface that promise pleasures of three-dimensionality: to produce a switch from actual reflec-

tion and absorption of light to implied warmth, pressure, sound, or odour. Fur is a substance with double capability to be all surface or all depth and so it can stand metaphorically for the two-way capabilities of naturalism. If the pleasure of the evocation of fur is linked, as it is here, to the reassuring presence of the mother then a socially endorsed response to maternal affection is annexed to the actual and implied sensory stimulation. The tender encounter of the polymorphously perverse infant with the maternal body is glossed as social as well as natural.

In Lance's picture of 1844, *Grandmother's Blessing,* there is a large area of quilted underskirt that occupies our attention as we gaze up at the presiding mother figure who sits making lace. This shares some of the characteristics of fur. It has the surface sheen of soft silk but the garment has the padded substantiality given by several layers of fabric that are sewn through in the quilting process. The lines of stitching signal depth, warmth and softness, while the flatter panels indicate the beauties of a reflective surface. The plump and spreading form of the lace-making cushion and the mother hen on the ground on the left pick up the theme of cushiony comfort. Everything in the picture speaks of plenty and fertility, though there is an insistence on virtuous work to preclude any suggestion of luxury and ease. Man and woman's work are symbolised by the garden fork and the spinning wheel on the right. In a post-lapsarian world virtue and survival are dependent on labour. A vine overhead bears clusters of grapes, a basket is full of potatoes, the mother has a sturdy son, the hen has produced a brood of chicks. The fruitfulness is initially replication. The church through the trees produces the pious grand-dame with her Bible and her blessing. She produces a daughter piously absorbed in her handwork. The mother produces a good child who is occupied throwing seed to the chickens. Again the themes converge with the capabilities of naturalism. Through naturalism it is possible to reproduce the actual. A second wooden horse can be produced in the reflective surface of the water. But the picture is prepared to talk about another kind of increase which is geometric rather than arithmetic, which has to do with transcending the limits of visual replication, which can mobilise the sentiments as well as satisfying the intellect. It is a kind of increase that is going to deliver satisfactions denied by the rigid repetition of this lifeless miniature from a man's world, this horse who has been led to water but can never drink.

The miracle of the grandmother's blessing is that from one wish so many different satisfactions can result. The picture offers a series of motifs that correspond to this miraculous increase. Arrayed around a heart on the cushion the lace bobbins spread out, weighting down the threads that the woman twists and separates in the making of lace. Arranged around each square on her quilted skirt are eight segments produced by the interweaving lines of stitching. In the bunches of grapes above her the plump and uniform fruit multiply in orderly clusters. On the ground beside her the hen sits at the centre of a circular array of little chicks. The child throwing birdseed might be said to be describing another reproductive circle. Rather than working as an image of virility and male potency, this boy spreading seed could be said to convey an idea of asexual reproduction. There is a shadowy father figure working in the distance on the left of the picture but the order of the picture is primarily maternal. Even where there is reference to a gendered division of labour: delving and spinning, male labour has produced a basket of potatoes. Male endeavour is subsumed within a model of asexual engendering. We do not see seed and its fruit but tubers that have developed around the mother plant, connected but detachable. Eve's spinning wheel with its radially connected spokes becomes identical rather than opposite to Adam's potatoes. The obliteration of sexual difference coincides with the ideological glossing over of social difference as the picture transports us imaginatively to a classless past. The group also suggests a Holy Family, and this too invites us to imagine parthenogenesis. Plenty and satisfaction in the picture are apparently produced by a process of splitting, whereby fragments of the mother's body are spread around her.

These offshoots share in the maternal substance but are detachable. A key concept here is the idea of the net, and the lace-making activity at the centre of the picture sets this out for us. From a nodal point the net extends in many directions. Different threads can be recombined to create another intersection. The pictorial evocation of sensory experience brings all the senses into a net in which sight is the junction. This is a kind of multiplying reproduction which goes way beyond the arid one-for-one replication of the mirror. The maternal body promises the exchange of sight for non-sight and offers a pleasurable interchange of senses and the experience of something beyond surface. The initial interchange makes possible the intricate patterning of a multiple sensory swap in which senses can be twisted and crossed over to produce lace. But the presence of the heart on the lace-making cushion is significant. The process is only satisfactory if the mother's heart is involved as well as her body: sentiment must enter into the interchanges as well as sensuality.[7]

If we return to the 'advanced' formulations of aesthetic experience we can see that not all commentators produced so rigid a separation between art and ethics as Whistler. Those writers who admit that aesthetics is based on physical response tend to see a continuity between art and life. This opens the door for ethical function through the action of emotion and empathy. The critic Philip G. Hamerton, for example, is quite clear about the sensory basis of art.

'The beginning of artistic aesthesis, or of that aesthesis which ultimately becomes artistic is simply animal sensation.'[8]

He talks of the relationship between taste in the artistic sense and in the gastronomic sense, and the way that the experience of the artistic involves, or approximates to, the animal sensations of flavour in the mouth, light and dark on the eye, or heat and cold on the body. He considers both the actual physiological response and the physical response produced by suggestion, or evocation. The aesthetic is, therefore, on a continuum with lower forms of physical sensation. In the aesthetic, though, those sensations are subtle and delicate, rather than crude, and are capable of awakening a huge range of emotions. Since there is a continuum between crude stimuli and sophisticated, refined stimuli, one has to ask where the aesthetic really starts. Hamerton goes back to the example of food and asks at what point

> '. . . the sensuousness of the hungry ploughman enjoying his slice of bacon is sublimated into the poetic rapture of Keats with a ripe peach melting in his mouth'.[9]

There is a difference between the basic, banal provision and the luxury fruit, between eating done automatically at the prompting of a healthy appetite and that done with deliberation for the sake of a heightened experience. Above all there is a difference between a rough ploughman and a refined poet. It is a class difference that underpins the transition from animal sensation to aesthetics. The desire and the ability to make fine discriminations between sense impressions depends on the level of culture. Hamerton implies that children, the lower classes and primitive peoples are driven by their appetites, while more educated individuals have sophisticated appreciation of the subtleties and emotional connotations of sense. He uses the example of colour. The love of *colours* is common among children and the 'undeveloped mind'. The linked appreciation of *colour* is reserved for those with more sophisticated faculties.

In this kind of aesthetic speculation we see a negotiation of the dangerous and undefined area between bodily sensation and higher functions such as rationality and spiritual experience. Sensation is dangerous because it links us to animals. On the other hand, as Eagleton has argued, aesthetics is developed to challenge untrammelled rationality. Sensory experience can be seen as a corrective to the overly abstract. Consequently the historical development of the aesthetic theory in the eighteenth and nineteenth centuries can be linked to a revaluation of the concrete, physical experience of individual bourgeois citizens as against the generalising abstraction of the absolutist regimes. Bourgeois societies are notionally based on free competing individuals. Aesthetics therefore has a universalising, democratic aspect insofar as it acknowledges the physiological aspects of the self.[10] In the second half of the nineteenth century aesthetics needed to tread carefully in this area so that it could maintain the ideological illusion of egalitarian democracy and yet preserve barriers to participation on the part of a threatening, animalistic working class.

Reading Leighton's *Addresses* we find that, like Hamerton, he sees a transition from sense, via form, to emotion. He conceives of sense impressions setting off emotional responses.

> 'We have within us the faculty for a range of emotions of vast compass, of exquisite subtlety, and of irresistible force to which Art and Art alone amongst human forms of expression has a key; these then, and no others, are the chords which it is her appointed duty to strike; and Form, Colour and the contrasts of Light and Shade are the agents through which it is given to her to set them in motion.'[11]

This is most important because it leaves open the door for subject matter and sentiment, and ultimately preserves the possibility of a didactic function for art. Figure painting necessarily offers a human focus for this emotion, and far from considering this an irrelevance or a distraction, Leighton enshrines this at the centre of his theory of art. The motifs of human life draw us in; the feelings aroused by the depiction of human situations form a crucial part of our response to art.

> 'In the emotion aroused by the phenomena of life, which we said was at the root of all Art, the central and culminating fact is our interest in Man; he is, and must be, the end and the means of whatever is greatest in the plastic Arts – as in every Art that tells of him; in the Art of Phidias, in the Art of Leonardo, in the Art of Homer, in the Art of Shakespeare.'[12]

It seems that on the terrain of emotion and human affairs the function of visual art is akin to that of literature. Laughter and tears, the warmth of affection and the solemn thoughts aroused by the phenomena of birth and death are fitting themes for art.

> 'Man's strength and beauty, his acts, heroic or homely, his gladness and his sorrow, his life and death – these are the materials in which painters and sculptors have ever found unfailing inspiration.'

It is this section of Leighton's *Addresses* that makes an argument for the centrality of sentiment. The empathic response of a human viewer to a human situation is not foreign to the purposes of art. Art does, in a certain way, function as a mirror, albeit one filtered through the temperament of the artist and presented through the formal means of art. The viewer recognises his or her own humanity in that mirror. In the act of recognition the individual is taken outside the enclosed existence of the 'free' social unit and, without coercion, forms a social bond. This is the ideological aspect of the aesthetic.

We should attend to the fragility of this moment of empathic identification. The position of sentiment is not unassailable because there is always the danger that it will give way to its artistically inferior cousin: sentimentality. The relationship of the visual arts to literature lies at the heart of the problem. Leighton describes the way that drama and fiction attract huge popular audiences because of the appeal of the passions of human existence. If art tries to transpose this source of interest directly, without working the passions through in formal terms, then it will remain impoverished and lacking in power. It will have some value, as long as it is sincere, but the most it can hope for is charm.

> 'The sincerity and directness of its expression is in Art an irresistible charm, and suffices to us in works in which the purely artistic quality is still feeble and undeveloped. The most deeply impressive works are those in which the human interest and the aesthetic quality are most fully blended.'[14]

The class distinction that we have already encountered in Hamerton's ploughman and poet operates here too. There is a spectrum of aesthetic worth from the charming to the deeply impressive. The masses are susceptible to charm and will respond to sentiment whether situations are depicted in literature or art. The sentiment that is depicted more powerfully, employing the proper means of art, is not crowd pleasing in the same way, it is possibly reserved for the cultured few. The illegitimate face of sentiment however is not that popular/literary manifestation but the insincere in which we do not recognise our humanity. It seems that truth is the test of sincerity. That which does not ring true is to be deplored. In such art there may be an appeal to the senses but there is nothing that speaks through the emotions of the human condition.

The point I want to emphasise is the inclusiveness of this aesthetic theory. There are degrees of worth and different ways of reading but the countenancing of humble genre scenes does not involve an abandonment of aesthetic criteria. It is a position that is, at once, socially and artistically inclusive, for all that it is informed by hierarchical systems. The danger signals for a critic to look out for are the artistically inept, the emotionally unconvincing and a stimulation of appetite rather than taste. Work may be not be great but it can still be worthwhile if it relies mainly on literary or anecdotal components and even if it depends on a relatively simple stimulation of sense. All work should affect the emotions of the viewer.

Modernist detractors of Victorian painting see only sentimentality where contemporary critics saw a complex orchestration of emotional response. A strong belief in the virtues of naturalism runs right through Victorian criticism. The endless variety of actuality was seen to offer an exhaustless supply of raw material for mounting fresh appeals to the finer feelings of the viewer. Emotion had to be freshly felt and could not be authentic in relation to the dull and formulaic. Critics complain about situations that are 'hackneyed' or 'threadbare'. A critic writing about Solomon's *Echo and Narcissus* in 1895 complained of the lack of originality in the presentation of the subject.

'In Mr. S. J. Solomon's "Echo and Narcissus" (770) the subject (which we hoped would never again appear upon canvas) is rather feebly conceived. Mr. Solomon is more demonstrative and sentimental than original or subtly sympathetic. Such tenderness and passion as the nymph's face expresses are to the point, but the rest of the picture is paint and prettiness.'[15]

In this case the critic is clearly looking for the emotion of the situation but feels that nothing new is being offered. The negative term 'sentimental' is being used in contradistinction to genuine sentiment. We need to attune ourselves to this kind of distinction in order to reconstruct the aesthetic experience offered by a collection such as that of the South London Art Gallery.

The involvement of the viewer's body while looking at pictures is an essential part of the process. Arguably Victorian audiences were less inhibited than modern art viewers. Since they expected to be touched by art they could expect to feel a glow of tenderness, a throb of pity, a stab of pain, the convulsion of laughter, or just the gradual realisation of a smile. Racing pulses, tingling nerves and muscular contraction were all part of the experience.

In the complex sensory and emotional switching that I have described, the physical response could mirror that of the subject or the picture could act as a kind of translating mirror. In viewing George Smith's *Sleeping Boot-Boy* the viewer does not yawn but feels mingled amusement and pity, a shade of disapproval and a tenderness in response to his relaxed vulnerability. Shades of feeling and combinations of response were to be managed, not just in dramatic situations of multi-figured action, where narrative identification governed response, but also in the banal inactivity or minimal incident of tame genre groups or single figures. Situations could be bitter-sweet, producing an agreeable turmoil in the viewer. The ambivalence between innocence and coquettishness might render a pretty figure intriguing.

The actual was thought to be the source of variety in sentiment as well as the guarantee against

George Smith, *The Sleeping Boot-Boy* (No. 57).

insincerity. Val Prinsep who is represented by a number of pictures in the South London Art Gallery wrote on this question in his Royal Academy Lectures of 1901 and 1902. He picks on the opposition between the real and the ideal in art and traces moves in society from idealism to realism, from the stern idealism of the early Greeks to the love of nature and worship of human beauty of the later period, from the religious sincerity and decorative feel of early renaissance art to the infusion of that religion with a sweet humanity in the work of Raphael, 'for sentiment was the characteristic of the new ideal', and from the vapid generalisations of the eighteenth century to the vigorous feel for nature in nineteenth-century work.[16] Sentiment is the necessary corrective to an overly generalised ideal. As he says, 'The ideal should be warmed into life by sentiment, for without it the ideal becomes cold and frigid'. Decorative qualities and harmonies of colour on their own can also be seen to be deficient where there is a lack of sentiment. He criticises Japanese art on this basis,

Val Prinsep, *An Unprofessional Beauty* (No. 49).

despite its artistic finish and sense of colour. He picks on the example of Albert Moore as an artist in whom the ideal has taken over. 'A hard-and-fast ideal is generally devoid of sentiment . . . The sentiment in Albert Moore's pictures is dead, whereas sentiment to impress the mind must be very living and supremely individual.' It is nature in all its variety that makes sentiment possible. In this context he makes a case for the aesthetic qualities of the retroussé nose.

'I see no reason, but rather a prejudice, why the straight, broad nose which is said to be Grecian, should be more beautiful than the delicate northern nose, which has even a slight tendency to be retroussé. Nay since it is the object of the artist to work on the emotions through the senses, the retroussé nose, and what is called irregular features, may be the more satisfactory, for the classic type is somewhat placid and cold.'[17]

This is reminiscent of Hamerton's amusing remarks on the relative aesthetic merits of the clean shaven face and the beard. He argues that shaving is inherently artificial and so appeals to those who favour the artificial, and value discipline, and he cites soldiers, lawyers and priests. Artists are credited with having originated 'the beard movement' and this is to be explained by their necessary feel for nature and its beauties.[18] This sort of discussion must lie behind Prinsep's intriguingly titled *Unprofessional Beauty*, shown at the Grosvenor Gallery in 1880. Does the delicate nose of this striking figure tend to the retroussé? The formalised beauties of the classical and Japanese-derived decoration behind her refer to formal beauties without sentiment, the soft and sleepy spaniel with its wrinkled nose to the attractive quirks and sentimental appeal of nature. The figure, who perhaps does not have the standardised beauty of a professional model, nonetheless combines elements of the ideal with the truth and the softening sentiment only available in nature.

Two mid-nineteenth-century genre works that dramatise and explore the sentimental capabilities of naturalistic genre employ the motif not of a mirror, as Lance does with his dish of water and toy horse, but that of a window. T. P. Hall's *One Touch of Nature Makes the Whole World Kin* of 1867 looks from inside an art dealer's window to the admiring crowd that has gathered on the pavement outside. Sophie Anderson's *No Walk Today* of 1856 views a little girl through a living room window from the garden. In Lance's work we saw three metaphors for naturalism: the mirroring water, the quilted skirt and the lace. The relationship between these is problematic. The water stood for a reduced and unemotional replication of the visual appearance of the world. The holes in the lace might be said to stand for transparent access through to the emotional intensities of the world. The picture does not present us with these though. Our primary focus is on the quilting which has no holes or windows, and so remains a surface like a picture. But it is a surface that has a depth, as the lines of quilting tell us. That depth effects a transition from the visual qualities of surface to the bodily sensations of warmth and softness. These sensual qualities give us access to a complex of pleasures, emotions and moral lessons associated with the mother's presence. The interest of the work however is that there is an acknowledgement that surface remains as a barrier to full emotional satisfaction. Along with the contentment of the scene there is a melancholy signalled by that diminutive, frozen horse.

Hall's art shop window frames a crowd which has been drawn together by the common factor of 'nature' in a picture on display. All the ages, both the sexes, and the different ranks of society are transfixed by the picture which we cannot see. The barriers that divide the gentleman from the manual worker, or the lady from the housemaid are overcome by the aesthetic experience. The close inspection of the gentleman and the slightly sour expression of the older lady suggest that youthful female beauty forms the subject of the picture. That female body offers a sensory experience that affects all these different social types in an unmediated way. As a result a unified social order coalesces. This is portrayed in the right hand window pane as the pretty young woman

Sophie Anderson, *No Walk Today* (Private Collection).

stands at the centre of an array of social types, from crossing sweeper to elderly gentlewoman. They are radially connected to her body. The notion is emphasised by the framing of another pretty young woman by the city omnibus door behind her. The omnibus is literally 'for all' people, and practically it serves all members of the public whatever their social station. This universal facility is shown to have beauty at its heart. The aesthetic, and nature which lies behind the aesthetic, are shown to be gendered female. In the interests of propriety the middle-class boy and the dandified gentleman are made to stand slightly apart and are framed by the next window pane. This slight reservation is the only concession the picture makes to any notion of naturalism being constrained by the limits of representation. It seems that the working-class males, and the elderly gentleman behind, can more easily be contained within the feminised sphere of aesthetic reproduction. The artist must have been well aware that,

actually, the crowding together of these ill-assorted social types would have caused great problems. The danger of moral or physical contamination from enforced proximity in the urban crowd was a familiar theme. This picture is about the miraculous abolition of the social differences that make the modern world so dangerous. The glass window in this picture is not used for a discussion of the difficulty of access to nature and sentiment but is considered simply in terms of transparency. We are given a celebration of the transparency of naturalistic art and the success of nineteenth-century genre in mobilising sentiment in the interests of a cohesive social order. The replication effected by naturalism is the reproduction of equal and interchangeable social units in a system that denies difference.

In Sophie Anderson's picture the extraordinary transparency of the glass brings us so close to the girl that we can see every detail of her figure. Textiles are given with great vividness, from the bulky folds of the matt walking dress, to the satin gleam of the jacket, the ironed flimsiness of the broderie anglaise collar, the brittle reflective texture of the straw hat and the fluffy softness of the ostrich feather on the hat. The perfection of the illusionism suggests to us that we could reach out and touch the child and feel these textures, but we are thwarted by the fact that, within the fictive space of the picture, the little girl is trapped behind the window. She cannot unflex her fingers and move them over the strut of the window frame. She can see but she cannot touch, smell or hear the outside world. Thanks to our supercharged vision we can see that her eyes have filled with tears, but her face shows no sign of a tear having dropped. Instead we see just a few raindrops trickling down the window surface outside. The picture is very precise about the mood of this little girl disappointed in her expectation of a walk by the inclement weather. We are not given gloom, fury or extravagant gestures but the restraint of sad contemplation in which the tears do not flow. The situation depicted offers some paradoxes. She is dressed up for going outdoors but is confined indoors. The outside where it is raining is bathed

T. P. Hall, *One Touch of Nature makes the Whole World Kin* (Private Collection).

in sunshine while the inside is cast in gloom. There are a number of parallels between interior and exterior. The sprays of jasmine that stray across the window almost seem to be looking in as she looks out. The motif of the little white jasmine flowers carries over into the interior where the little flowers of her lace collar, and the individual blossoms of lilac on the net curtains echo them. The glossy sheen of the wet shrubs at the edge of the windows is echoed by the sheen of her blue-green jacket. But none of these rhymes is complete. The green is not a match for the green of the shrubs. The lilac on the curtains seems large and clumsy in comparison to the delicate forms of the jasmine and, of course, it has no scent. Their juxtaposition stresses the clumsy artificiality and the sensory deprivation of the interior. The girl is a living natural thing like the flowers outside, but she is caught in a world of surrogates. Vision is her only link to the natural world outside, just as it is the picture viewer's only means of access to the

multiple sensory experience of nature. Further than this it is a barrier to complete emotional experience. The gap between the brimming eyes and the trickling raindrops is narrow, art can approach life, but it is nonetheless an impassable barrier. Our empathic feeling for the child is channelled into a feeling of regret for the impossibility of truly swapping between the senses. Sophie Anderson's picture harnesses the sentimental capabilities of genre to a melancholy reflection on the limits of representation.

Samuel Carter's *Rabbits* can be seen to participate in the ideological work of naturalism in the way that it speaks directly of motherhood and in the way its evocation of fur maintains the possibility of rubbing both ways and so switching between the senses. The myths of aesthetic generation supported by the picture are complicated by the very explicit thematisation of the possibilities of selective breeding. These settled rabbits are the very opposite of the shy and wary wild breed. Wild rabbits were discussed in terms of their constant alertness and readiness to flee, their erect ears able to pick up the slightest sign of danger, their white tails acting as alarm signal when the first rabbit in a group took off. Even their warrens in which the tunnels channelled and amplified sound were likened to ears. The nineteenth-century texts on the rabbit, whether from a naturalist's angle or from the point of view of hunting or maintaining warrens for profit, emphasise their timidity, their ability to breed prolifically and the damage they can cause to crops. R. O. Edwards calculated, roughly, that, since one pair of rabbits could produce 240 young in a year, the resulting rabbit population 'if allowed to multiply with freedom' would number 1,800,000 in five years. In times of low yield it seemed profitable in many areas to put land over to maintained warrens and to profit from the meat and the fur of these creatures. At other times the crop damage caused by rabbits led to desperate efforts to control them, ranging from trapping, ferreting and shooting to more extreme efforts at extermination: poisoning crops (soaking them in alcohol or painting them with arsenic), experimenting with viruses from 1887 and, from the 1910s, employing mustard gas and cyanide gas in warrens. There was ongoing friction between the sporting interests of landowners and the efforts of tenants to protect crops. The rabbit was considered the most democratic of foods since it was eaten by every rank from farmhand to noble, but the social tension over poaching and shooting rights was considerable. The Ground Game Act of 1880, known as the Rabbit and Hare Bill, was a fairly unsuccessful effort to solve these disputes.[20] Against this background of open violence and class conflict the possibilities for anthropomorphising depictions of cuddly bunnies were somewhat limited. How could this marauding pest with libertine breeding habits and a cowardly disposition to turn tail become the object of emotional identification? Beatrix Potter's rabbit stories are remarkable for the way they face up to the violence and conflict of the countryside. Through the dynamic of the dramatic situation she makes possible an identification, not with the good bunnies, but with the reprobate Peter and Benjamin and takes us through their fearsome encounters with the murderous farmer. Works of popular science did their best by emphasising the exceptional moments when rabbits forgot their timid natures and defended their young. J. E. Harting's *The Rabbit* of 1898 recounts instances of mother rabbits seeing off stoats, weasels and crows, and accompanies these anecdotes with a plate labelled *Maternal Instinct*, in which we see the mother rabbit carrying her baby in her mouth and hopping to the safety of the burrow entrance.[21]

The tame rabbit, by contrast, was marked by its docility and containability, and offered a suitable subject for genre painting.[22] Landseer's painting of 1839 *Children and Rabbits* showing a boy and a girl cuddling and feeding pet rabbits was a popular work engraved in 1842 and in 1874. Frederick Morgan who painted touching scenes involving children and animals from the 1870s painted a scene called *Alice* in which a little girl in pink feeds frilly cabbage leaves to a large group of fluffy white rabbits. This is the safe normality of Alice when she has woken up from her crazy and perplexing dream. Domestic rabbits live overground in

Children and Rabbits, engraving after Landseer.

hutches which are subject to the inspection and the environmental control of the rabbit keeper. Rabbit fanciers' handbooks of the period are filled with discussion about the most effective and economical means of providing heating and ventilation for the hutches. Their breeding can also be limited to a moderate two to three litters a season. Family sizes can be controlled by using foster mothers so that valuable does only keep four or so young (the best specimens) and the others are cared for by foster mothers of a less valuable breed and can be fattened for the table. All this translates very easily into the terms of the social policy of an interventionist state, or the measures proposed by paternalist philanthropy. The late nineteenth century was a period when the British state took fears about the degeneration of the race very seriously and were prepared to investigate the danger of the physical decline of the working class as breeding stock. The impact of Social Darwinism meant that commentators were ready to transfer

Frederick Morgan, *Alice* (Unilever Historical Archive).

Maternal Instinct, from J. E. Harting's *The Rabbit*.

observations from the animal kingdom into the context of human society. Darwin himself had made extensive observations on domestic rabbits, among other domestic animals, in his investigations into selective breeding in *Variations of Animals and Plants Under Domestication* published in 1868.

In terms of rabbit breeding the subject of Samuel Carter's *Rabbits* is the premier breed. R. O. Edwards in a handbook of 1884 says 'The lop-ear has often been termed the Prince of all rabbits, and to look at it with all its handsome properties who could say that it has been else than rightly named?'[23] J. Rogers in *Rabbits and their Habits* of 1885 describes the lop-ear as 'the most prized, the most valuable and the most sought after' of rabbits. Prices for good specimens could be as high as £20. It was also the largest breed, occasionally reaching over sixteen pounds in weight, and regularly weighed over eleven pounds. Lop-ears were described as the most English of breeds. Prize rabbits were produced by careful crossing. Lop-ears could be shown in a number of different categories depending on their colouring and markings. Breeders sought to develop uniform shades and symmetrically marked animals in two colours, with clearly divided colours, avoiding spotty and mottled effects. In a litter not all the young would develop the lop ears and not all the lop-ears would have the very long ears desirable in show animals. They were also concerned to produce generally strong and healthy specimens – judging did not depend on ear length alone.[24] If we attempt to moralise Carter's picture, with this kind of information in mind, we can see the rabbits here as examples not only of the advantages of motherly love but as examples of the benefits of environmental control and the possibilities of improving the breed. With the right conditions the English worker can be made bigger, stronger, tamer and more handsome.

The brood is miscellaneous. The variety of fancy breeds was celebrated and linked specifically to domestication.

'The wild rabbit, as we are well aware, continues to retain, while in a state of natural liberty, the same peculiarity of form, size and colour that has always distinguished its ancestral race . . . No sooner however does man capture or decoy them from the warren, the field, the wood, or the forest, and rear and bring them up under his subjection, than the effects of domestication begin to exhibit themselves in the endless variety which is the sure consequence of his breeding, rearing and feeding.'[25]

The plain coloured bunny in the foreground of the picture is clearly exhibition material and has reproduced all the fine characteristics of the mother. The two spotty examples with uneven ears are not very impressive, but the markings on the fawn and white pair nearest to the mother's head are full of possibilities. To produce a lop-ear with these markings through cross breeding would be worthwhile. The picture offers us nature with all its variety, but it is nature tamed and approachable. It is also a nature that has been aesthetically enhanced. It proposes an aesthetic formula that, like Prinsep's *Unprofessional Beauty*, improves upon the ideal by introducing the infinite, random variety of nature, and improves upon the appealingly natural by introducing the symmetries and grandeur of the ideal.

Alongside the aesthetic formula there is a social formula. At one level these well-behaved and contented rabbits offer a straightforward equivalent to the working class audience that the organisers of the South London Art Gallery wished to see. If the first lop-ear breeding club could be established in the Woolwich, Plumstead and Charlton region in 1850 then why could not the neighbouring inhabitants of Camberwell take the lessons of selective breeding to heart in the 1890s? In the intervening forty years the improvement of the breed had been dramatic. These fine rabbits stand for the achievements of the present and the boundless possibilities of the future.

There does seem to be an equivocation between these targeted resonances of the image that rest precisely on the notion of sexual difference and sexual reproduction, and the sensory magic of aestheticised fur. These small furry creatures work universally on the sentiments of viewers. I would argue that it is not an adult instinct for protecting small mammals that is activated. Rather it is a promise of access to a fantasy world of asexual reproduction. These bunnies cluster around the gigantic doe as tuber-like fragments of an extensive and spreading maternal body to which we can all imagine equal access. Variety is not then the result of crossing but the sign of the multi-sensory pre-Oedipal satisfactions.

In Landseer's *Children and Rabbits* the domesticated creatures are overseen by a boy and a girl. The boy has one rabbit, probably the buck, restrained in a cloth. The girl is cuddling the other adult rabbit, probably the mother, holding the furry pet up to her face. These two actions relate to the twin ideological functions of this and many other touching genre images. First there is the capability of instructing and disciplining the onlooker through emulation or repulsion. This is associated with masculinity and sexual reproduction. Secondly there is another kind of emotional instruction which is associated with femininity and with the multiple stimulation of the senses. These contradictory forms of access to the subject are, however, not offered as alternatives. Successful genre painting with maximum sentiment has it both ways.

The efforts of genre painting are directed to the production of sentiment. It is only possible to produce sentiment if the impression can be maintained that the senses are equal but different. Social and sexual difference is, similarly, inscribed and denied in the ideological work of naturalism. Modernist austerity has made it difficult to attend to the range of physical and emotional response mobilised in Victorian genre. My argument has been that we must recover those responses in order fully to understand the aesthetic qualities and the ideological functioning of Victorian sentimentality.

FOOTNOTES

1.   T. Eagleton, *The Ideology of the Aesthetic*, 1990.
2.   J. A. M. Whistler, 'The Action', *The Gentle Art of Making Enemies*, 1890. For a recent account of the trial see Linda Merrill, *A Pot of Paint: Aesthetics on Trial in Whistler v. Ruskin*, 1992.
3.   'Mr. Whistler's Ten O'Clock', in Whistler, 1890.
4.   Joseph A. Kestner, 'Poynter and Leighton as Aestheticians: The Ten Lectures and Addresses', *Journal of Pre-Raphaelite and Aesthetic Studies*, vol. II, no. 1, Spring 1989, pp.108-120.
5.   E. J. Poynter, *Ten Lectures on Art*, 1880, p.84.
6.   1887 catalogue cited in Borzello, 1987, p.71.
7.   This analysis of the image draws on Kristeva's notion of a connection between the pre-Oedipal experience of the maternal body and the sensory aspects of aesthetic experience. See J. Kristeva, *Desire in Language*, edited by L. S. Roudiez and translated by A. Jardine et al., 1980. I am arguing that those aesthetic pleasures, far from escaping ideology, or offering an anti-ideological space, as Kristeva's early work suggests, are vital to the ideological working of sentiment.
8.   P. G. Hamerton, *Portfolio Papers*, 1889, p.169.
9.   ibid, p.173.
10. Eagleton, 1990.
11. Sir F. Leighton, *Addresses Delivered to the Students of the Royal Academy*, 1896, p.55.
12. ibid, p.16 (1879).
13. ibid, p.19.
14. ibid, p.17.
15. *Athenaeum*, 22 June 1895, p.811.
16. V. Prinsep, *Lectures Delivered to the Students of the Royal Academy of Arts of London*, 1902, p.44.
17. Prinsep, 1902, p.53, p.34, p.51.
18. Hamerton, 1889, p.189.
19. R. O. Edwards, *Rabbits for Exhibition, Pleasure and the Market*, 1884, p.25.
20. John Sheail, *Rabbits and their History*, 1971. Sheail comments on the opposition to the use of gas when the horrors of gas warfare became known. The parallel between rabbits in warrens and men in the trenches was readily made (p.182).
21. J. E. Harting, *The Rabbit*, 1898, plate opp. p.20. William Davis, *A Field of Green Corn*, c.1860, uses rabbits in the foreground in an unusual way to emphasise the seclusion and tranquillity of a corner of the field, see C. Payne, *Toil and Plenty: Images of the Agricultural Landscape in England 1780-1890*, 1993, p.117. The graphic violence of Landseer's *The Feast Interrupted*, 1838, links more readily to the conflict described in the nineteenth century. The dead hare and uprooted turnip fill the foreground while a snarling ferret stands in the background. Illus., W. Cosmo Monkhouse, *The Works of Sir Edwin Landseer . . .*, 1879.
22. Popular natural history texts, such as J. G. Wood, *Glimpses Into Petland*, 1863, and *Petland Revisited*, 1884, drew moral lessons from the humble and familiar creatures of the backyard.
23. Edwards, 1884, p.53.
24. L. U. Gill, *The Book of the Rabbit*, 1881. The environmental measures taken to alter form included corrective caps made from leather straps to even out ears that pointed at the wrong angle.
25. J. Rogers, *Rabbits and their Habits*, revised W. Heath, (24th edition), 1885.

Sunday Evening at a South London Picture Gallery

'The crowd in the Walworth Road, from which the visitors to the humble "Gallery" were drawn, were boisterously gay, but pitifully sad to look upon. Under-sized factory girls with pale over-strung faces, under gaudy beflowered and feathered hats, set off with plush Directoire coats and tawdry satin paletots, with imitation jewellery in profusion, hustled each other in hoydenish fashion or marched to the time of a rollicking comic song. At one moment they would join in a coarse and loud guffaw; at another, would attract the attention of a group of men by a well-planned collision. Here were young girls of fifteen walking hand in hand with lads of the same age, who strutted with the dignity of bantam cocks, while they made love to the puffing of cheap cigars. Other girls there were who carried little babies in their arms, and had a hunted, hungry look in their eyes, that told an all-too-plain tale. Men, stunted, pale, hollow-eyed "mouched" along with trouser-pocketed hands, and lads, tired and old-looking, shouted under the railway arches or roared out fragments of Salvation Army Hymns. At last I got to the Picture Gallery. "Do these people appreci-ate the pictures?" I asked of the young lady atten-dant. "Not at first, they have to come a few times, and then they begin to understand them better." "Do you get many visitors?" "We average 4,000 weekly attendance, and 2,000 on Sunday; but we had 845 this afternoon, which is larger than usual, and we have had many more to-night on account of the Baroness's collection." "And you have no difficulty in keeping order?" "Sometimes we have a little trouble, but as a rule they are extremely well-conducted." "You close on Saturdays, I see?" "Yes; we take our Sunday then, as it is a slack day. It would not do to close on Sundays here, so many people would be disappointed." On the whole the little South London Fine Art Gallery is well worth a visit, and whatever doubt might have been in my mind before as to the rightness of opening these "places of recreation" on Sunday, I came to the conclusion that so far as I had been able to judge, this was the only successful rival I had found to the public-house.'

From the *Pall Mall Gazette*, 14 October 1889

WORK IN FAITH   FAITH IN WORK.

The Catalogue

edited by Robert Maniura

Objects are listed according to the original owners. These have changed in some cases. The South London Art Gallery changed its name to South London Gallery in 1992. The collection of the Ancoats (or Horsfall) Museum is now held in Manchester City Art Galleries. Unless otherwise stated, the object is in the collection of the South London Gallery.

LIST OF ABBREVIATIONS

R.A.	Royal Academy
S.L.A.G.	South London Art Gallery
S.K.	South Kensington
N.G.	National Gallery
S.P.P.	Society of Portrait Painters
G.G.	Grosvenor Gallery
R.C.A.	Royal College of Art
P.R.A.	President of the Royal Academy

SOUTH LONDON ART GALLERY

Maurice Bingham Adams (1849-1933)

Architect. Became editor of Building News *in 1872 and undertook many projects for the proprietor, J. Passmore Edwards, including the Passmore Edwards Libraries at St. George's in the East (1897), Acton and Shepherds Bush (1899) as well as the Camberwell Polytechnic (1896-98). Involved in the creation of Bedford Park, Chiswick, he gained an international reputation.*

3

1 *South London Art Gallery*

Pen and ink on paper, 64 x 84 cm

SIGNED AND DATED: *Maurice B. Adams FRIBA, Architect & Delt, Feb 1902*

Adams exhibited the design at the R.A.

Presented by the architect

2 *South London Art Gallery, Elevation of Peckham Road Façade, End Elevation and Roof Plan*

Watercolour and pen on paper, 49 x 66.5 cm

SIGNED AND DATED: *Maurice B. Adams FRIBA, Architect, Chiswick, London W, May 1896*

Southwark Local Studies Library

Charlotte E. Babb (fl.1862-91)

Based in London, Miss Babb regularly exhibited genre and mythological subjects. Probably related to J. S. Babb, whose work is also represented at S.L.A.G.

4

3 *Yesterday, Today, Tomorrow*

Oil on canvas, 101.5 x 127 cm

SIGNED AND DATED: *Charlotte E. Babb 1891*

The passage of time is personified by three female figures. Yesterday turns away, petals falling from her fading flowers. Today confronts the viewer bearing a cup. A freshly dug trench and a spade separate her from Tomorrow, who appears with face covered and led by a child. The crow's call can be read as 'cras, cras' ('tomorrow' in Latin).

Carl Bauerle (1831-1912)

A German artist who came to England as portrait painter to Prince Albert. A regular exhibitor at the R.A., he occasionally painted genre and landscapes.

4 *The Toy Shop*

Oil on canvas, 81 x 66 cm

SIGNED: *C. Bauerle*

Presented by the artist

Henry John Boddington (1811-65)

Born Henry Williams into a family of painters, the artist adopted his wife's surname to avoid confusion and establish an independent reputation. He exhibited at the R.A. from 1837 until his death.

5 *Sketch From Nature*

Oil on canvas, 35.5 x 54 cm

Presented by Miss Julia Duckworth

Thomas Brock R.A. (1847-1922)

Trained at R.A. Schools, he worked in John Foley's work-shop and completed several of the sculptor's commissions after his death. Assisted Leighton in his sculptural projects and later designed his tomb in St. Paul's Cathedral.

6 *Lord Leighton*

Bronze bust, 38 cm high

INSCRIBED: *Thos. Brock R.A. Sculp. 1892*

Ford Madox Brown (1821-93)

Born in Calais and trained in Bruges and Antwerp. Committed to the idea of art for the working man, he helped set up a drawing school for artisans at Camden Town and taught at the Working Men's College 1858-61. Closely associated with the Pre-Raphaelite Brotherhood, he also worked for a time as designer in William Morris' firm.

Studies for The Body of Harold brought before William the Conqueror

The large cartoon for which these drawings are studies was Brown's entry to the 1844 competition for the decoration of the Houses of Parliament. Rejected by the Parliamentary commissioners, the cartoon remained in the artist's collection. It was purchased by the Madox Brown Fund Committee and presented to the South London Art Gallery, in 'acknowledgement of the generous efforts made by Sir Frederic Leighton and Mr G. F. Watts on behalf of the Gallery'. The cartoon reveals the artist's schooling in continental history painting and the studies clearly show the laborious method involving nude studies of each individual figure.

7 *A Wounded Soldier*

Charcoal on paper, 43 x 57 cm

8 *A Monk*

Charcoal on paper, 45.5 x 40 cm

These figures were singled out in a description of the cartoon Brown gave in a letter, reprinted in the 1895 catalogue:

'A fair haired Norman officer, regardless of the fact that his body is gashed pretty freely with wounds, twists about to get a sight of Harold. The monk who is dressing his wounds, tired out with much of such work, surlily bids him to be quiet.'

9 *Two Soldiers Carrying the Body of Harold*

Charcoal on paper, 58.5 x 42 cm

Ford Madox Brown, *The Body of Harold brought before William The Conqueror*, before war damage.

10   *Three Heads*

Charcoal on paper, 54.5 x 75 cm

The three heads are all represented in the final cartoon. The one at the bottom left is the head of the standing soldier at the left of the finished composition. That on the right is the head of the figure immediately to his right and the third is that of the central figure, turning to look at William.

Katharine Bruce (1858-1927)

Niece of the author and scholar Anna Swanwick (1813-99) who donated her pictures to S.L.A.G. Her work was also exhibited at Whitechapel in 1891.

11   *The Five Foolish Virgins*

Oil on canvas, 139.5 x 51 cm

The picture illustrates the parable in Matthew's Gospel. The Whitechapel catalogue provided the following text:

'"And the door was shut." ST. MATT. xxv.10.

"No light had we: for that we do repent:
And hearing this, the bridegroom will relent -
Too late! too late! ye cannot enter now.
No light: so late! and dark and chill the night!

11

O let us in, that we may find the light!
Too late, too late: ye cannot enter now.'"

12 *The Cup of Death*

Oil on canvas, 84 x 41 cm

The Whitechapel catalogue gave the following description:

'A girl standing by the brink of a river. An Angel holds the Cup of Death, while the girl's pleading, sorrowful eyes seem to ask to be spared the bitter draught. But the Angel points upward and her calm strength imparts courage.

"So when the angel of the darker drink,
  At last shall find you by the river brink,
  And, offering his cup, invite your soul
  Forth to your lips to quaff, you shall not shrink."
                From the Rubaiyat of Omar Khayyam.'

Presented by Miss A. Swanwick

Albert Bruce-Joy (1842 - 1924)

Eminent Irish sculptor, known for his portraiture, full-size public statues and smaller busts and statuettes. Attended S.K. and R.A. Schools and was trained in the 'naturalistic' style by John Foley.

13 *Portrait Profile of a Lady*

Moulded plaster, circular, diameter 30 cm

14 *Portrait Profile of Professor George Gabriel Stokes (1819-1903)*

Moulded plaster, oval, 40 x 35 cm

Stokes was a celebrated mathematician and physicist, known especially for his work on the motion of viscous fluids. His investigations of optics led him to the discovery of fluorescence and of the invisible ultra-violet spectrum.

16

William Cater Bull (fl.1890s)

Streatham painter. Exhibited atmospheric landscapes at venues in London.

15 *Quiet Evening from Brighton Pier*

Watercolour on paper, 24.5 x 41 cm

SIGNED: *W. C. Bull*

Presented by the artist

Cecil Leonard Burns (1863-1929)

Painter of portraits, mythological figure subjects, genre and flowers. Studied under Herkomer. Exhibited at R.A. Jointly Principal of Camberwell School of Arts and Crafts and Curator of S.L.A.G. (1897-99). Later Principal of Bombay School of Art.

16 *Lady at Needlework*

Pastel on canvas, 91 x 76 cm

17 *Invitation to the Opening of South London Art Gallery, 6 June 1898*

Southwark Local Studies Library

John Wilson Carmichael (1800-68)

Newcastle-born. Travelled extensively along the coastline of Britain, painting along the way. War artist during the Crimean war, his studies were used for engravings in the Illustrated London News. *Author of two books on marine painting.*

18 *Dover*

Oil on canvas, 40 x 84 cm

Presented by Mrs Barclay

Samuel John Carter (1835-92)

Norfolk-born artist who specialised in animal paintings. Studied at the Norwich School of Design and the R.A. Schools. Exhibited at the R.A. Ruskin described one of Carter's works as capturing 'a moment of supreme puppy felicity' in his 1875 Academy Notes.

19 *Rabbits*

Oil on canvas, 51 x 68.5 cm

SIGNED AND DATED: *Samuel Carter 1872*

Presented by Sir Henry Gooch

F. G. Coleridge (fl.1866-1891)

Berkshire landscape artist. Exhibited widely in London.

20 *Near Henley*

Watercolour on board, 18 x 27 cm

Presented by Miss Duckworth

21

The Hon. John Collier (1850-1934)

Second son of the 1st Lord Monkswell, himself an amateur landscape painter. Studied at Eton, the Slade, Paris and Munich. Exhibited at the R.A., the N.G. and the S.P.P., of which he was President. Painted mainly portraits and subject pictures.

21 *A Devonshire Orchard*

Oil on canvas, 101.5 x 129 cm

SIGNED AND DATED: *John Collier 96*

Charles Collins (fl.1867-1903, d.1921)

Landscape and animal painter. Studied at the West London School of Art. Exhibited widely.

22 *Two Studies of a Stream*

Oil on canvas, each section 12 x 17 cm

Presented by the artist

23

Walter Crane (1845-1915)

Painter, illustrator, and designer of textiles and wallpapers. Influenced by Burne-Jones and the Pre-Raphaelites, he associated with Morris in the Socialist League. Exhibited at the R.A. and G.G. Principal of the R.C.A. 1898-99.

23 *The Triumph of Labour*

Wood engraving, 38 x 84.5 cm

SIGNED: *Designed and drawn by Walter Crane. Engraved by Henry Schell*

Print issued to celebrate May Day 1891. Crane described the work in his *Artist's Reminiscences:*

'The design . . . represented a procession of workers of all kinds, both manual and mental, marching out to celebrate the International May Holiday, and bearing banners and emblems declaring their ideals . . . As the print was to be issued simultaneously in different countries, I rewrote the mottoes in French and German, and I think Italian also. William Morris told me he thought it "the best thing I had done."'

Presented by the artist

24 *Corona Vitae*

Wallpaper filling, colour print from wood blocks, 93.5 x 52 cm. Produced by Jeffrey & Co., 1890.

Crane explained:

'The design may be understood as generally emblematic of a full, rich and ample life, not without its changes and contrasts, but ever springing anew to flavour and fruition. While the floral winged lions, supporting the Crown of Life, indicate its material triumphs; the sphinxes on either side of the tree, figure its mystery, and those unanswered problems perpetually presented afresh to humanity in the fruit of the Tree of Knowledge.'

Lewis Foreman Day (1845-1910)

Trained in France and Germany, he set up independently as a designer, his work covering the whole field of applied art. Also a lecturer and writer on design, he was a founder member of the Artworkers' Guild.

25 *Wallpaper filling with a design of formalised camellias*

Colour print from wood blocks, 111 x 54.5 cm. Produced by Jeffrey & Co.

Tristram Ellis (1844-1922)

A scientist who studied at King's College, London, he turned to painting watercolour landscapes. Travelled widely in Europe and the Near East. Exhibited frequently at the R.A. 1868-1904 and published Sketching from Nature *and* On a Raft and Through the Desert, *a travel book illustrated with his engravings.*

26 *View of the Needles and Freshwater Bay, Isle of Wight*

Watercolour on paper, 23 x 51.5 cm

SIGNED AND DATED: *Tristram Ellis 1886*

Presented by the artist

27 *The Giants Causeway*

Watercolour on paper, 23.5 x 53 cm

Presented by the artist

Axel Haig (1835-1921)

In Sweden Haig studied ship-building and moved to Glasgow to find work. He moved to London and joined a firm of architects. Under Ewan Christian and William Burgess he developed expertise in architectural drawing and Gothic detail, later becoming a full-time artist. He travelled extensively, preparing large plates of Gothic buildings for publication. Exhibited at R.A.

28 *Westminster Abbey*

Etching, 66 x 54.5 cm

One of a series of three etchings by Haig of Westminster Abbey in the collection.

Presented by W. H. Pollock

Charles Edward Hallé (1846-1919)

Son of the famous conductor Sir Charles Hallé. Studied with Baron Marochetti and Van Mottez. Best known as a portraitist, he was a co-founder of the N.G. and G.G.

28

29 *Quentin Durward*

Oil on canvas, 94.5 x 52.5 cm

Quentin Durward is the eponymous hero of a novel by Sir Walter Scott set in fifteenth-century France. A Scottish soldier in the service of the French king, Durward is assigned to protect a fleeing Burgundian heiress, finally winning her hand.

Presented by the artist

Viscount Hardinge (1822-94)

Painter of landscapes and buildings. Exhibited widely.

30 *Abbeville*

Watercolour on paper, 34 x 24 cm

Presented by the artist

31 *A Forest Scene*

Watercolour on paper, 24 x 34 cm

Presented by the artist

Frederick Hamilton Jackson (1848-1923)

Studied at the R.A. Schools and became Master of the Antique School at the Slade and Principal of Chiswick School of Art (designed by Maurice Adams). Taught at the R.A. Schools. Interested in craft and design, he wrote on marquetry and mural decoration.

32 *Garden in Chiswick*

Watercolour on paper, 52 x 36 cm

SIGNED AND DATED: *F. Hamilton Jackson 1884*

Presented by the artist

33 *Old Church in Malden*

Watercolour on paper, 31 x 53 cm

SIGNED AND DATED: *F. Hamilton Jackson 1885*

Presented by the artist

J. R. Jaques (fl.1882-87)

London painter. Exhibited at Society of British Artists.

34 *Headland*

Watercolour on paper, 14 x 19 cm

SIGNED AND DATED: *J. R. Jaques 87*

Presented by the artist

32

34

Frederic, Lord Leighton P.R.A. (1830-96)

Studied in Florence, Rome, Frankfurt, Brussels and Paris. Patronised early in his career by Queen Victoria, he rose to become perhaps the central figure of the art establishment, accorded the unique honour of a peerage shortly before his death.

35 *Massacre of the Innocents*

Oil on board, 33 x 30 cm

A sketch after the painting by Bonifazio Veronese now in the Accademia, Venice.

Presented by Lady Frampton

36 *Wedded*

Engraving, 51 x 24 cm

Based on the oil painting of 1881-82.

Presented by the artist

37 *Meditation*

Engraving, 38 x 24 cm

Presented by the artist

38 *Innocence*

Engraving, 38 x 28 cm

Presented by the artist

36

Thomas Rose Miles (fl.1869-88)

Painter of seascapes and landscapes. Exhibited at R.A. 1877-78.

39 *The Return of the Lifeboat*

Oil on canvas, 76 x 127 cm

SIGNED AND DATED: *T R Miles 1879*

The 1895 catalogue commented:

'A Londoner can scarcely realise the excitement of a life boat going out to a ship in distress, still less of its return with those it has saved from the wreck. The people who stand on the shore, unable to help, can only wait and hope, while the boat goes out at great danger to its crew, in hopes of carrying safety to others. The return is the crowning moment of excitement, everyone eager to know what good work has been done.'

Presented by S. P. Thompson

C. E. Minifie (fl.1890s)

40 *Swanage Bay*

Oil on canvas, 33 x 53 cm

SIGNED AND DATED: *C. E. Minifie, 1892*

Presented by the artist

Evelyn de Morgan (1855-1919)

Studied under her uncle, Roddam Spencer Stanhope, and at the Slade and in Italy 1875-1877. Her meticulous technique is based upon the painters of the Italian Renaissance, especially Botticelli, and her subject matter is derived from the Bible, mythology and mediaeval romance. Burne-Jones influenced her later work. Exhibited at the G.G. and N.G. Married William de Morgan in 1887. G. F. Watts described her as 'the first woman artist of the day'.

41 *The Christian Martyr*

Oil on canvas, 216 x 91 cm

This is one of de Morgan's largest canvases. Its subject probably derives from the story of Margaret Wilson of Wigtownshire (1667-85), a member of a strict puritan sect, sentenced to drowning in the Solway for refusing to acknowledge the Episcopacy. Millais painted versions of this subject in 1862, 1863 and 1870. Unlike Millais, who depicted Margaret in plausible seventeenth-century dress, de Morgan shows the figure wearing distinctly un-puritan scarlet draperies, presumably symbolising martyrdom. The meaning of the inscripton 'NAZARAEA' above her head is not clear.

William de Morgan (1839-1917)

The leading ceramicist of the Arts and Crafts Movement and friend of the Pre-Raphaelites. Studied at R.A. Schools. He provided many decorative tiles in an Eastern style for Leighton's house. Abandoned pottery about 1905 because of failing health and became a novelist.

42 *Ceramic Tiles*

The tiles date from the early years of the Fulham pottery 1888-97, although some of the designs had already been in production before this time.

'Pineapple'
Four tiles, each 15.25 cm square

Conventionalised Flower Design
Four tiles, each 15.25 cm square

'Carnation'
Two tiles, each 15.25 cm square

'Gillow'
Two tiles, each 15.25 cm square

'Bedford Park Anemone'
Two tiles, each 15.25 cm square

Design with Leaves and Berries
Two tiles, each 15.25 cm square

Bertha Newcombe (fl.1876-1904)

Painter based in Croydon. Member of the Society of Lady Artists, she exhibited at R.A.. A Fabian, she was for a time romantically involved with George Bernard Shaw.

43 *Waterlilies*

Oil on canvas, 45.5 x 48 cm

SIGNED AND DATED: *Bertha Newcombe 1886*

Presented by the artist

Marianne North (1830-90)

Travelled worldwide painting nature studies and landscapes. Most of her oils are housed in a specially built gallery at Kew Gardens, opened in 1882.

44 *Wild Flowers From Monte Ceneroso*

Oil on paper, 21 x 25.5 cm

Alfred Parsons R.A. (1847-1920)

Regarded as a quintessentially English artist and noted for his expert paintings of gardens. Studied at the S.K. School. Exhibited regularly at R.A. from 1871. Worked widely as an illustrator. Elected President of the Royal Society of Painters in Watercolour in 1913.

45   *American Apple Orchard*

Oil on canvas, 131 x 85.5 cm

SIGNED AND DATED: *Alfred Parsons 1882 New York*

William Carpenter bequest

46   *Morning on the Kennet*

Oil on canvas, 77 x 51 cm

SIGNED AND DATED: *Alfred Parsons 1880*

Presented by the artist

Valentine Cameron Prinsep R.A. (1838-1904)

Studied with Watts and collaborated with Rossetti and Burne-Jones on the Oxford Union murals and other projects. Also worked with Leighton, a neighbour in Holland Park Road, and Millais. A popular and successful figure, he became Professor of Painting at the R.A. Schools in 1900.

47   *The Death of Siward the Strong*

Oil on canvas, 184.5 x 251 cm

Exhibited at the R.A. and the Liverpool Academy in 1882. Siward, Earl of Northumberland, was the warrior who led the army which defeated Macbeth. He died at York early in 1055. The 1895 catalogue explained:

'Earl Siward desired to die with his armour on and in the open air. When he was dying his family respected his wishes by putting on his armour and carrying him out that he might not die in a house.'

Presented by the artist's executors

48

48   *Medea, the Sorceress*

Oil on canvas, 142.2 x 111.7 cm

Exhibited at Whitechapel in Spring 1891. The catalogue entry read:

'Medea, a famous witch of the old Greek stories, is here seen gathering toadstools and poisonous herbs to make her magic charms. Many stories are told of the wonders she did, as when she composed an ointment for her lover, which, when applied to his body and shield, preserved him from all harm.'

The S.L.A.G. catalogue of 1895 gave:

'Medea was the daughter of Ætes, king of Colchis, a celebrated magician. She was the wife of Jason. By her power she restored Jason's father to youth, and did many other wonderful deeds.'

Presented by the artist's executors

49 *An Unprofessional Beauty*

Oil on canvas, 91.4 x 71.1 cm

Presented by the artist's executors

Thomas Matthews Rooke (1842-1942)

Trained at the R.C.A. and R.A. Schools. Became a designer in William Morris' firm and was appointed assistant to Burne-Jones. Chosen by Ruskin in 1878 to make drawings of cathedrals and other important buildings in Europe. In his early years he specialised in biblical subjects painted in the manner of the Pre-Raphaelites and developed a characteristic method of illustrating a narrative in a number of scenes, framed together, showing successive events in the story. Jephthah's Daughter *is a fine example.*

50 *Jephthah's Daughter*

Oil on canvas, 91 x 121 cm including frame. Side scenes 57 x 27.5 cm, central scene 57 x 36.5 cm

The story appears in Judges 11: 30-40. Jephthah led the Israelites against the Ammonites. He made a pact with God that, in return for victory in a crucial battle, he would sacrifice the first living creature that came to meet him in the aftermath. The Israelites were victorious, but his daughter was first to greet him. The five scenes were described as follows in the 1895 catalogue:

'1 Jeptha [sic] vowing to sacrifice the first person he met after victory
2 Jeptha gaining the victory
3 Jeptha's daughter coming first to meet him
4 Jeptha's daughter mourning
5 The sacrifice'

Presented by the artist

51 *Elijah Reproving Ahab*

Oil on canvas, 101 x 126 cm

SIGNED AND DATED: *T M Rooke 1878*

Exhibited at Whitechapel in spring 1892. The catalogue gave this explanation:

'Ahab, the king, coveted the vineyard of Naboth, who would not sell it to him. Jezebel, Ahab's wife, and his evil genius, obtained it from him by the unjust execution of its owner.

"Then the word of the Lord came to the prophet Elijah saying: Arise, go down to meet Ahab, King of Israel. He is in the vineyard of Naboth, whither he has gone down to possess it. And thou shalt speak unto him saying: Thus saith the Lord, hast thou killed and also taken possession? In the place where the dogs licked the blood of Naboth shall dogs lick thy blood, even thine."

Elijah is delivering his message. The masterful queen, thwarted but unabashed, is as full of suppressed passion as the prophet. Between them, the shamed king is shaken; his limbs, his face, the wavering poise of his whole body tell that the prophet will triumph. The sunny sky, the profusion of fruit, say "Give", but Ahab has taken, and reaps the wrath of the just man.'

Presented by Lord Battersea

John Ruskin (1819-1900)

Noted principally as a writer and critic, he was a considerable draughtsman, his works reflecting his analytical approach to art and nature. Increasingly concerned with economic and social issues he published a series of monthly letters, Fors Clavigera, *'to the workmen and labourers of Great Britain' and founded the Guild of St. George whose members gave a tithe to philanthropic purposes.*

52 *Study of a Column Capital at Assisi*

Watercolour and graphite on coloured paper, 21.5 x 16 cm

53 *Portion of a Screen*

Watercolour and ink on coloured paper, 26.5 x 29 cm

54 *Limestone Cliffs of the Wengen Alp*

Graphite on paper, 23.5 x 29 cm

INSCRIPTION: *Limestone cliffs of the Wengen Alp from Lauterbrunnen (1846)? J. Ruskin signed 23rd Dec 78*

52

George Smith (1829-1901)

Genre painter who specialised in domestic scenes with children. Exhibited extensively.

57   *The Sleeping Boot-Boy*

Oil on canvas, 35.5 x 30.5 cm

Solomon Joseph Solomon R.A. (1860-1927)

Studied at the R.A. Schools and in Munich and Paris. Exhibited extensively at the R.A.. Produced pictures with themes taken from the Bible, classical antiquity and northern legend as well as portraits. Elected president of the Royal Society of British Artists in 1918.

58   *Matthew Wallace, 1st Mayor of Camberwell*

Oil on canvas, 92 x 72 cm

Wallace was Mayor at the time that S.L.A.G. became the property of the Borough of Camberwell.

Presented to the Borough by a body of subscribers

55   *Copy of an Illumination from the Book of Kells*

Watercolour on paper, 10 x 18.5 cm

Everton Sainsbury (1849-85)

London genre painter. Exhibited widely.

56   *Superstition*

Oil on canvas, 122 x 153 cm

SIGNED AND DATED: *Everton Sainsbury*

Exhibited at R.A. in 1883. The picture was accompanied by a verse:

'Down in the crimson west the sun had sunk
Amidst the tattered fragments of the storm.
Oh, all ye sweet things of transparent day
Hasten from night and its grim visitants.'

Henry Scott Tuke R.A. (1858-1929)

A leading member of the New English Art Club. Specialised in painting the male nude in the open air. Studied at the Slade and in Paris, where he was influenced by the French plein-air *painter Jules Bastien-Lepage.*

59   *Boy's Head*

Oil on canvas, 45.5 x 30.5 cm

Presented by the artist

60   *Boy Drinking*

Oil on canvas, 23 x 16 cm

Presented by the artist

60

Sir Ernest Albert Waterlow R.A. (1850-1919)

Landscape and animal painter in oils and watercolour. Studied in Heidelberg and Lausanne and at R.A. Schools.

61 *Early Morning in the Thames Valley*

Oil on canvas, 37.5 x 59.5 cm

SIGNED AND DATED: *E A Waterlow 1881*

Presented by the artist

George Frederic Watts R.A. (1814-1904)

Celebrated but not always understood by his contemporaries, he is now remembered chiefly for his portraits rather than the ambitious, large-scale allegories upon which he staked his reputation. His Gallery survives at Compton, Surrey.

62 *Lord Leighton*

Etching, 33 x 24 cm

SIGNED AND DATED: *G F Watts 1880*

Related to the oil portrait of 1881 now in the National Portrait Gallery.

63 *The Open Door*

Oil on canvas, 126 x 65.5 cm

SIGNED AND DATED: *G F Watts 1892*

Exhibited at Whitechapel in spring 1893 and at S.L.A.G. in 1895. The Whitechapel catalogue gave the following description:

'The maiden has opened the door to look at the storm and a white butterfly flies in search of shelter. A butterfly – Psyche – was the Greek symbol for the soul. Does the picture mean that into the maiden's soul also the butterfly of hope, of awakening love, will shortly enter, or that a soul, tossed by the storms of passion, finds refuge in the home of innocence and peace?'

William Morrison Wyllie (fl.1852-95)

London painter of genre. Exhibited widely. Represented by a large number of works at S.L.A.G. The 1895 catalogue listed 'thirty-four studies' by the artist.

64 *Fishing Boat Scene*

Oil on board, 15 x 33 cm

65 *Fishing Boat Scene*

Oil on board, 13 x 35.5 cm

Unknown Artist

66 *John Wilkes (1727-1797)*

Oil on canvas, 39.5 x 34 cm

Political radical and defender of parliamentary privilege in the eighteenth century.

ANCOATS MUSEUM

Formerly known as the Manchester Art Museum or Horsfall Museum. Founded in 1884 by T. C. Horsfall and transferred to Ancoats Hall in 1886. Collection now in the possession of Manchester City Art Galleries.

Basil Bradley (1842-1904)

Son of a Manchester portrait painter. Studied at Manchester School of Art and exhibited regularly in Manchester and London.

67 *A Red Squirrel Eating a Nut*

Oil on millboard, 30.5 x 22.8 cm

SIGNED: *B Bradley*

Léon-Émile Caille (1836-1907)

Born in Merville, near Lille, Caille was taught by Cogniet. He painted genre scenes and exhibited in both Paris and London.

68 *Prayer*

Oil on Panel, 16 x 10.5 cm

SIGNED AND DATED: *Léon Caille, 1872*

Mothersill bequest, 1880

Randolph Caldecott (1846-86)

Illustrator and watercolourist. Studied at Manchester School of Art and Slade. His work was featured in various publications including Punch *and* The Graphic, *but he is best known for his children's book illustrations. He described his work as 'the art of leaving out as a science'. Caldecott's work was shown in the* Mother's Room, *intended primarily for the enjoyment of children.*

69 *Illustrations for* **The Three Jovial Huntsmen, Picture Book No. 5, 1880.**

Sketch of the Three Jovial Huntsman Riding Across a Field

Pen and brown ink on paper, 7.7 x 13.3 cm

Sketch of the Three Jovial Huntsman Linking Arms

Pen and brown ink on paper, 7.7 x 13.3 cm

Sketch of the Three Jovial Huntsman on Horseback Galloping Across a field

Pen and brown ink on paper, 7.7 x 15.6 cm

Sketch of the Three Jovial Huntsman Riding Across a Field With a Church in the Background

Pen and brown ink on paper, 7.6 x 11.4 cm

William Holman Hunt (1827-1910)

Member of the Pre-Raphaelite Brotherhood. Studied at R.A. Schools where he met Millais. Visited the Middle East in 1854, 1869 and 1873 in search of accuracy for his religious paintings. Remained true to the principles of the Brotherhood, producing elaborately detailed paintings and prints until the end of his life.

70 *Triumph of the Innocents*

Engraving, 40.5 x 32.5 cm, wooden frame with illuminated vellum designed by Charles Robert Ashbee (1863-1942)

This is the 'beautifully framed copy of some edifying picture' commissioned by T. C. Horsfall from the Guild of Handicraft. This guild was set up in 1888 by C. R. Ashbee, the arts and crafts architect and designer. Ashbee was responsible for the illuminated lettering of the Ruskin quotation, and the wooden frame was made by fellow guild member, C. V. Adams.

John Ruskin (1819-1900)

71 *Head of Adam from the Façade of the Ducal Palace, Venice*

Graphite with watercolour on paper, 34.6 x 26.5 cm

William Wyld (1806-89)

Began his career as a diplomat, working as secretary to the British Consul in Paris. Turned to art and established a reputation as a landscape and topographical painter. Based in Paris, he exhibited in France and England.

72 *St Cloud*

Pencil, watercolour and bodycolour on buff paper, 31.5 x 24.4 cm

SIGNED: *W Wyld*

INSCRIBED: *St Cloud. Augt 71*

73-76 are characteristic examples of the decorative art objects acquired at modest cost by Horsfall as demonstrations of good design: many of these were reproductions.

73 *Priam asking Achilles for the body of Hector*

Wedgwood blue jasperware plaque, 21.5 x 44.5 cm, late nineteenth century

First modelled by Pacetti in the 1780s, the design is based on a sarcophagus in the Capitoline Museum in Rome.

Presented by Charles Rowley

74 *Jug*

Tin glazed earthenware, painted underglaze in blue, pewter mount, Delft, 1884, height 21.5 cm

75 *Vase*

Earthenware, painted underglaze with copper and cobalt, Jaipur School of Art, Delhi, 1880s, height 31.75 cm

Presented by Mr Ashton, 1889

76 *Vase*

Bronze, Naples, nineteenth century, height 26.7 cm, diameter 13.3 cm

Copy of a Pompeian bronze vessel.

77 *T. C. Horsfall*, **An Art Gallery for Manchester, 1877**

78 *T. C. Horsfall*, **The Manchester Art Museum, 1878**

79 *C. Rowley*, **Fifty Years of Work Without Wages, 1911**

Manchester Central Library

GUILD OF ST. GEORGE

Founded in 1870 and funded by a 'tithe' from its members, the guild was involved in the running of the museum at Walkley, set up in 1875 and taken over by Sheffield Corporation in 1890. The collection of the guild is now held in the Ruskin Gallery in Sheffield.

Louise Virenda Blandy (1860-90)

A pupil of Ruskin from the age of 13, she began to assist him in copying in the 1880s. Exhibited at the Grafton Galleries 1879-81.

80 *Seven Angels in the Resurrection (after Fra Angelico)*

Watercolour and bodycolour with gold on paper, 17 x 25.7 cm

A study of figures from the predella panels, now in the National Gallery, London, of Fra Angelico's altarpiece for San Domenico di Fiesole. Possibly executed in 1883-4 on a direct commission from Ruskin.

Charles Fairfax Murray (1849-1919)

Pre-Raphaelite painter who was taught by Rossetti and was an assistant to Burne-Jones. He was sent by Ruskin to Italy to copy Old Masters of which this drawing is an example. He was also an art dealer and an important collector and left bequests to many museums including Dulwich.

81 *Nativity (after Botticelli)*

Watercolour on paper, 33.5 x 23 cm

Thomas Matthews Rooke (1842-1942)

82 *Study of mosaics in the Altar dome of the Baptistery of St. Mark's, Venice, representing the Principalities and Powers in Heavenly Places*

Watercolour, bodycolour and gold on paper, 65.5 x 70.5 cm

One of the studies commissioned by Ruskin as part of his campaign to record the unaltered state of important monuments threatened by 'restoration'. The mosaics of St. Mark's were being gradually replaced by modern copies but the scheme was abandoned in the face of international pressure. Executed in 1879, this was one of the few watercolours to survive a fire on the train returning from Italy which destroyed the bulk of Rooke's Venetian work.

83 *View of the East End of Chartres Cathedral from the river Eure*

Watercolour and bodycolour on paper, 30 x 31 cm

The visit to Chartres in 1885 was the third of the four expeditions Rooke undertook for Ruskin. It resulted in some of the artist's finest architectural water-colours. Ruskin approved: 'Nothing has ever yet been done in expressive architectural painting like Mr. Rooke's porches and windows of Chartres.'

84 *Primavera (after Botticelli)*

Chromo-lithograph on paper, 53 x 82.3 cm

Produced by the Arundel Society

Arthur Burgess (d.1887)

An assistant to Ruskin. A wood engraver by training, he was used extensively after 1869 to measure and annotate architecture.

85 *Detail of Rouen Cathedral*

Photograph

One of the photographs taken as part of a survey of the West Front of Rouen cathedral which Burgess directed for Ruskin in 1880.

86 *Spiral Carving from the North West Portal, Rouen Cathedral*

Plaster cast, 107 x 54 cm, 1880s

87 **William White, *The Principles of Art, 1895***

White was Curator of the Ruskin Museum.

88 *Fors Clavigera*

Pamphlets published by George Allen, 1871-7.

89 *Selection of semi-precious stones*

Brecciated Agate, Quartz enclosing large needle-like crystals of Rutile, Selenite containing Hematite, Calcite of the Dog Tooth variety, Clear Quartz, Amethyst lining an Agate Geode, Specular Iron and Quartz, Labradorite, Agate Nodule and Geode with crystals of Quartz, Calcite and Manganese Dioxide.

WHITECHAPEL ART GALLERY

The first loan exhibitions were organised by Samuel Barnett in St. Jude's School, Whitechapel, in 1881. A scheme for a permanent gallery was launched in 1897 and the new building, designed by Harrison Townsend, opened in 1901.

90 *Catalogue of Whitechapel Fine Art Loan Exhibition, Easter 1887*

91 *Catalogue of Whitechapel Fine Art Exhibition, Easter 1891*

92 *Catalogue of Whitechapel Fine Art Exhibition, Easter 1892*

93 *Catalogue of Whitechapel Art Gallery Winter Exhibition, 1901-2*

94 *Handbill for Whitechapel Art Gallery Spring Exhibition, 1901*

95 *Sermons of the Revd. Lucking Taverner*

Booklet of press cuttings

96 *Drawing class at Myrdle Street School*

Photographic print, 1908

97 *Interior of Whitechapel Art Gallery, Spring Exhibition 1901*

Photographic print

TOYNBEE HALL

Founded in 1884, the Universities Settlement was a prototype 'University' of East London where young men from Oxford and Cambridge lived and worked to provide education and recreation for the poor.

Sir Hubert von Herkomer R.A. (1849-1914)

Born in Bavaria; his family settled in England in 1857. Studied at S.K. School under Sir Luke Fildes. Exhibited extensively from 1869. A successful portraitist, he also produced landscapes and genre pictures with a strong vein of 'social realism'.

98 *Samuel and Henrietta Barnett*

Oil on canvas, 147.5 x 99 cm

Presented to the Barnetts on 20 November 1908 at a ceremony in Toynbee Hall with Asquith as the principal speaker. The portrait shows Samuel Barnett standing beside his wife who studies plans of Hampstead Garden Suburb.

99 **Henrietta Barnett,** *Canon Barnett: His Life, Work and Friends,* 1918

100 **Charles Booth,** *Life and Labour of the People in London,* 1885-1902

101 *The Toynbee Record, 1882-92*

HORNIMAN MUSEUM

Frederick John Horniman, tea tycoon, amassed a large and varied collection from his travels and worldwide contacts which was kept in his house on Surrey Mount. The collection was opened to the public in 1890. A new building was commissioned from Harrison Townsend in 1898 and on its completion in 1901 the museum was given 'to the people of London'.

R. P. Gossop

102 *The Horniman Free Museum*

Watercolour on paper, 93 x 76 cm

SIGNED AND DATED: *R P Gossop 1901*

103 *Shells from the collection of John Morgan*

John Morgan (1782-1854), philanthropist and writer, devised projects similar to those of Robert Owen of Lanark, but more avowedly Christian. In 1849 he founded the National Orphan Home in London. Morgan's collection of shells was exhibited at S.L.A.G. in the 1890s.

104 *Selection of natural history items including birds, fish, ostrich eggs, butterflies and moths*

CUMING MUSEUM

These objects come from the important collection assembled for the Cuming Museum (now London Borough of Southwark). They illustrate the type of decorative arts acquired for S.L.A.G.

105 *Commemorative mug*

Earthenware mug, Doulton, 1887

Commemorates Queen Victoria's golden jubilee.

106 *Staffordshire sugar vase*

Wedgwood jasperware-style 'semi-porcelain' earthenware, Dymock of Hanley, 1822

107 *Export china mug*

Hard paste porcelain mug made in China for the European market, c.1780-1800

108 *Roman pottery urn*

Sepulchral urn of black burnished ware, c.AD 100-300

109 *Roman brick*

Hollow incised earthenware brick, c.AD 100-300

Found in the City of London.

110 *Nepalese kukri*

c.1850

Traditional broad-bladed knife with a leather scabbard, carried in Nepal.

SOUTHWARK LOCAL STUDIES LIBRARY

111 **Books and Pamphlets**

A Short History of the South London Fine Art Gallery, 1896

Elizabeth Rossiter, Founder of Country Life for Poor Town Children. A Memorial, 1890

South London Art Gallery Catalogue, 1983

South London Art Gallery, *Weekly Notes on Art, Nature, Literature and Science,* 1891-2

Borough of Camberwell, *South London Art Gallery,* leaflet, c.1900

Invitation to Laying of Foundation Stone, 30 July 1896

CAMBERWELL COLLEGE OF ARTS

112 **Books**

Camberwell School of Arts and Crafts, Prospectuses 1898-1908

Walter Crane, *The Claims of Decorative Art,* 1892

Lewis F. Day, *Nature in Ornament*

Select Bibliography

A Description of the Work of the Manchester Art Museum, Ancoats Hall, 1895

W. Besant, *All Sorts and Conditions of Men*, 1882

C. Booth, *Life and Labour of the People in London. 3rd Series: Religious Influences. Outer South London*, 1902

F. Borzello, *Civilising Caliban: The Misuse of Art 1875-1980*, 1987

A. Burton, *The Bethnal Green Museum of Childhood*, 1986

Department of Science and Art, *Annual Reports*

T. Eagleton, *The Ideology of the Aesthetic*, 1990

P. G. Hamerton, *Portfolio Papers*, 1889

M. Harrison, 'Art and Philanthropy: T. C. Horsfall and the Manchester Art Museum' in *City, Class and Culture*, eds. A. Kidd and K. Roberts, 1985

M. Harrison, 'Ancoats Art Museum' in *Manchester Region History Review*, VII, 1993

T. C. Horsfall, *An Art Gallery for Manchester*, 1877

T. C. Horsfall, *Handbook to the Manchester Art Museum*, 1886

Sir F. Leighton, *Addresses Delivered to the Students of the Royal Academy*, 1896

J. Macdonald, *Passmore Edwards Institutions*, 1900

H. Meller, *Leisure and the Changing City*, 1976

L. and R. Ormond, *Lord Leighton*, 1975

V. Prinsep, *Lectures Delivered to the Students of the Royal Academy of Arts of London*, 1902

The Works of John Ruskin, eds. E. T. Cook and A. Wedderburn, 1907:
    vol. XIII, 'Picture Galleries - Their Functions and Formation', 1857
    vol. XIX, 'Modern Art', 1867
    vol. XXXIV, 'A Museum or Picture Gallery: Its Function and Its Formation', 1880

E. Russell Barrington, *The Life of Lord Leighton*, 1906

M. Watts, *George Frederic Watts*, 1912

J. A. M. Whistler, *The Gentle Art of Making Enemies*, 1890

MATERIAL FROM THE SOUTH LONDON ART GALLERY ARCHIVES

Plan of Buildings and Guide of South London Art Gallery, 1894

Catalogue of Works of Art in the Gallery, South London Art Gallery and Lecture Hall, 1895

South London Fine Art Gallery and Free Library, Report for 1886

South London Fine Art Gallery and Free Library, Report for 1887

South London Fine Art Gallery and Free Library, Report for 1891

South London Fine Art Gallery, Report of a Public Meeting held on 18 July 1890

W. Rossiter, *A Summary of the History of the South London Art Gallery, Library and Lecture Hall, from its Foundation in 1868, a Quarter of a Century Ago*, 1893.

W. Rossiter, *Weekly Notes on Art, Nature, Literature and Science*, November 1891.

OTHER ARCHIVAL MATERIAL

Camberwell School Prospectus, 1898

Minutes of the London County Council Advisory Sub-Committee of Camberwell School of Arts and Crafts (Camberwell College of Arts archives)

DULWICH PICTURE GALLERY

Art for the People
Dulwich Picture Gallery, 27th April-26th June 1994

Front Cover: Thomas Rooke, *Elijah Reproving Ahab* (South London Gallery)

Back Cover: Samuel Carter, *Rabbits* (South London Gallery)

Catalogue edited by Giles Waterfield and Robert Maniura, and designed by Barry Viney

© Dulwich Picture Gallery, London, 1994

Printed in England by The Lavenham Press, Water Street, Lavenham, Sudbury, Suffolk CO10 9RN

ISBN 1 898519 02 1